UZBEKISTAN

BAHRAIN

CYPRUS

IRAN

IRAQ

ISRAEL

JORDAN

KUWAIT

LEBANON

OMAN

QATAR

SAUDI ARABIA

SYRIA

TURKEY

UNITED ARAB EMIRATES

YEMEN

AFGHANISTAN

BANGLADESH

BHUTAN

INDIA

NEPAL

PAKISTAN

SRI LANKA

MALDIVES

CHINA

JAPAN

MONGOLIA

SOUTH KOREA

NORTH KOREA

TAIWAN

HONG KONG

BRUNEI

MYANMAR (BURMA)

CAMBODIA (KAMPUCHEA)

LAOS

MALAYSIA

SINGAPORE

THAILAND

PHILIPPINES

VIETNAM

ALGERIA

BENIN

BURKINA FASO

CAMEROON

CAPE VERDE

CENTRAL AFRICAN REPUBLIC

CHAD

DJIBOUTI

EGYPT

The
STUDENT WORLD ATLAS

text by JULIA GORTON

illustrated by NICHOLAS PRICE

LODESTAR BOOKS

Dutton   New York

Editors: Julia Gorton and Angela Royston
Editorial Assistants: Kim Kremer and Lakshmi Hughes
Designers: Maggie Aldred and Cathy Tincknell
Design Assistant: Julie Marston
Picture Researcher: Emily Hedges
Production Controller: Ruth Charlton

Library of Congress Cataloging-in-Publication Data

George Philip & Son.
    The student world atlas / illustrated by Nicholas Price; text by
Julia Gorton.-1st American ed.
        p.   cm.
    Originally published in Great Britain in 1994 by George Philip
Limited as Philip's picture atlas for children.
    Includes index.
    ISBN 0-525-67491-8
    1. Children's atlases. [1. Atlases.] I. Price, Nick (Nicholas
R.), ill. II. Gorton, Julia.   III. Title.
G1021.G490 1994 <G&>
912--dc20   94-16288
                                                              CIP
                                                          MAP AC

First published in the United States in 1994 by Lodestar Books, an
affiliate of Dutton Children's Books, a division of Penguin Books USA
Inc., 375 Hudson Street, New York, New York 10014

Originally published in Great Britain in 1994 by George Philip Limited,
an imprint of Reed Consumer Books Limited, Michelin House, 81
Fulham Road, London SW3 6RB, and Auckland, Melbourne, Singapore
and Toronto

Printed in Italy by LEGO SpA

First American edition

ISBN 0-525-67491-8

10 9 8 7 6 5 4 3 2 1

CONTENTS

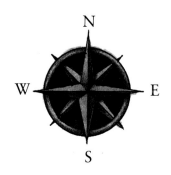

INTRODUCTION
WHAT IS A MAP? 4
HOT AND COLD PLACES 6
LOOK CLOSER! 8
COUNTRIES OF THE WORLD 10

MAPS
WESTERN EUROPE 12
EASTERN EUROPE 14
SCANDINAVIA 16
RUSSIA AND THE NEW INDEPENDENT STATES 18
THE MIDDLE EAST 20
SOUTH ASIA 22
EASTERN ASIA 24
SOUTHEAST ASIA 26
NORTHERN AFRICA 28
SOUTHERN AFRICA 30
CANADA 32
THE UNITED STATES 34
CENTRAL AMERICA AND THE WEST INDIES 36
SOUTH AMERICA 38
AUSTRALIA 40
NEW ZEALAND AND THE PACIFIC 42
ANTARCTIC 44
ARCTIC 45

INDEX 46
QUIZ ANSWERS 48
ACKNOWLEDGEMENTS 48

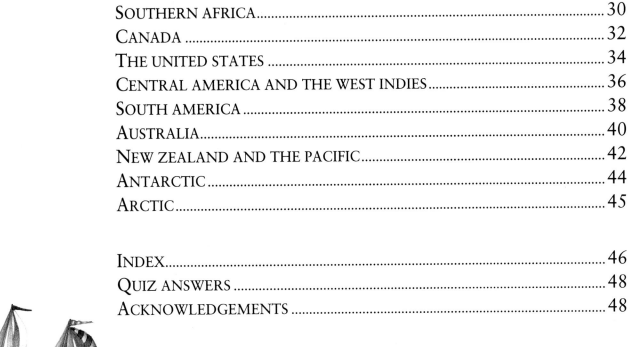

WHAT IS A MAP?

From space, the Earth looks like a huge, round ball, covered mostly by water and partly by land. The shape of each piece of land and sea, and the names we give to them, can be shown on a map. Maps give a kind of picture of the Earth's surface, as if we were looking down from above. The detail shown on a map depends on how far above the surface the "picture" was taken.

If you were orbiting Earth in a satellite, you could look down and see the whole of Africa. But, except for the highest mountains and the biggest lakes, you would not be able to see much detail. ▼

Shrinking to fit

```
0     20    40    60    80    100   120   140  feet
0     5    10    15    20    25    30    35   40  meters
```

▲ A map is a small picture of a big area, so everything it shows has to be shrunk to fit in. This diesel locomotive is really nearly 15 meters long, but here it's less than 30 millimeters. It has been scaled down, and the scale bar tells us by how much - 10mm or 1cm in the drawing represents 5 meters on the ground.

◀ Here, the scale bar shows that the picture covers a wider area, as if we were looking at the train from farther away. Now, 1cm on the drawing represents 50 meters on the ground, so the train looks much smaller.

```
0    200   400   600   800   1000  1200  1400  feet
0   50   100  150  200  250  300  350  400  meters
```

▶ If you look down on the scene from above and from farther away again, you can't see actual objects at all. Now we need to use labeled symbols, as on a true map.

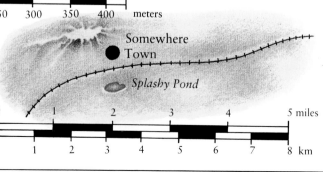

Somewhere Town

Splashy Pond

```
0      1      2      3      4       5 miles
   1    2    3    4    5    6    7    8 km
```

Flat maps of the Earth, ▶ which show all the land and sea at once, are very useful. But it is not easy to make a flat map of a round object. Map makers have special ways of doing this. Sometimes, they have to stretch and bend the land shapes to make them fit into the area they want, so the actual shapes shown are not as accurate as they are on a globe.

North Pole

EUROPE

AFRICA

Equator

ATLANTIC OCEAN

South Pole

A globe is a map that shows the land and sea on a round ball. It shows exactly where the continents and oceans are positioned, as well as the names we give to different places. A globe might also show the pretend lines that map makers use to divide up the Earth's surface. One of the most important is the Equator, the dotted line around the middle of the Earth halfway between the North and South poles.

· POINTING · THE · WAY ·

N

W   E

S

You will see this symbol on every map. Like a compass needle, N always points to the North Pole and north is always at the top of the map. South is at the bottom. The compass shows that east is always on the right and west on the left side of the map.

Arctic Circle

NORTH AMERICA

EUROPE

ASIA

Tropic of Cancer

ATLANTIC OCEAN

AFRICA

PACIFIC OCEAN

PACIFIC OCEAN

Equator

INDIAN OCEAN

SOUTH AMERICA

Tropic of Capricorn

AUSTRALIA

Antarctic Circle

ANTARCTICA

HOT AND COLD PLACES

It is always hot around the Equator and cold at the North and South poles. Some parts of the Earth get plenty of rain, but some get hardly any rain at all. Different climates suit different kinds of plants and so produce different environments for animals and people to live in. The map opposite shows you the main environments in the world. Apart from the Countries of the World map, all the maps in this book use these colors to show the different environments.

Spreading the sunshine

Sunshine spreads thinly across the ground at the poles. It is always cold here, especially in winter.

The farther you go from the Equator, the colder it gets. Countries between the tropics and the poles have warm summers and cold winters.

Sunshine is strongest in the tropics, between the lines on the map called the Tropic of Capricorn and the Tropic of Cancer. The climate here is always hot, with wet and dry seasons.

Arctic Circle

Tropic of Cancer

Equator

Tropic of Capricorn

Although there are thick forests at the foot of these mountains, no plants at all grow on their peaks. This is because the air gets colder and colder as you get higher up.

Very few plants or trees can survive in deserts like this because the blazing sun is too harsh and the sandy soil is too dry.

A forest of pine, spruce and other evergreen trees stretches as far as the eye can see. The huge evergreen forests in Canada and northern Asia and Europe are called the taiga. The taiga of northern Asia is the largest forest in the world.

It is so cold in the Arctic and Antarctic that even parts of the sea freeze over. Ice that floats on the surface of the sea is called pack ice. In the short polar summer, some of the pack ice melts, but it soon freezes again as the long, bitter winter sets in.

Icy places/ mountain ranges

Evergreen forest

Desert

Tropical rain forest

Woodland

Grassland and scrub

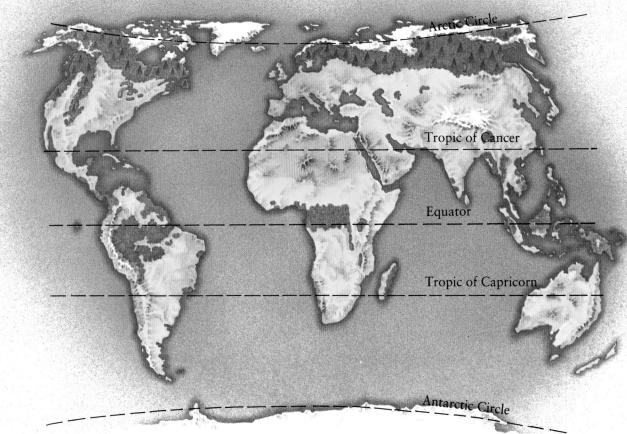

Arctic Circle

Tropic of Cancer

Equator

Tropic of Capricorn

Antarctic Circle

Plants grow so thickly in tropical rain forests that it is almost dark near the ground. The air here is hot and damp. Some rain forest trees can reach as high as 40 meters or more. Twisting creepers grow up and around their trunks to get a share of the sunlight.

Natural grassland is too dry for many trees to grow, but it is good for grazing animals and farming crops.

7

LOOK CLOSER!

Maps try to show you as much as possible about the huge areas they represent, but they can only fit in the most important cities and the biggest rivers, lakes and mountains. Look at the small pictures to find out more about each country. They tell you how the people live, what they eat, the kinds of things that they make, and what plants and animals are usually found there. The pictures are not, of course, drawn to match the size of the other things on the map. A whole city is shown just by a dot, but beside it you may see a picture of a single, famous building in that city.

All countries have farms. Some of the pictures on the maps show the kinds of crops that are grown or the types of animals that are raised. Rice, one of the main food crops in China, is grown in special, flooded fields called paddies.

Red pandas, like this one, live in bamboo forests in the mountains of southwestern China. Look out for pictures of wild animals on all the maps. You'll see that the type of animal you find depends on both the landscape and the weather of each different area.

These children are wearing brightly colored, embroidered kimonos, the traditional dress of Japan. You'll find pictures of traditional dress on many of the maps. They show the kinds of clothes that people in that area wear, sometimes for everyday use, but more often for special occasions.

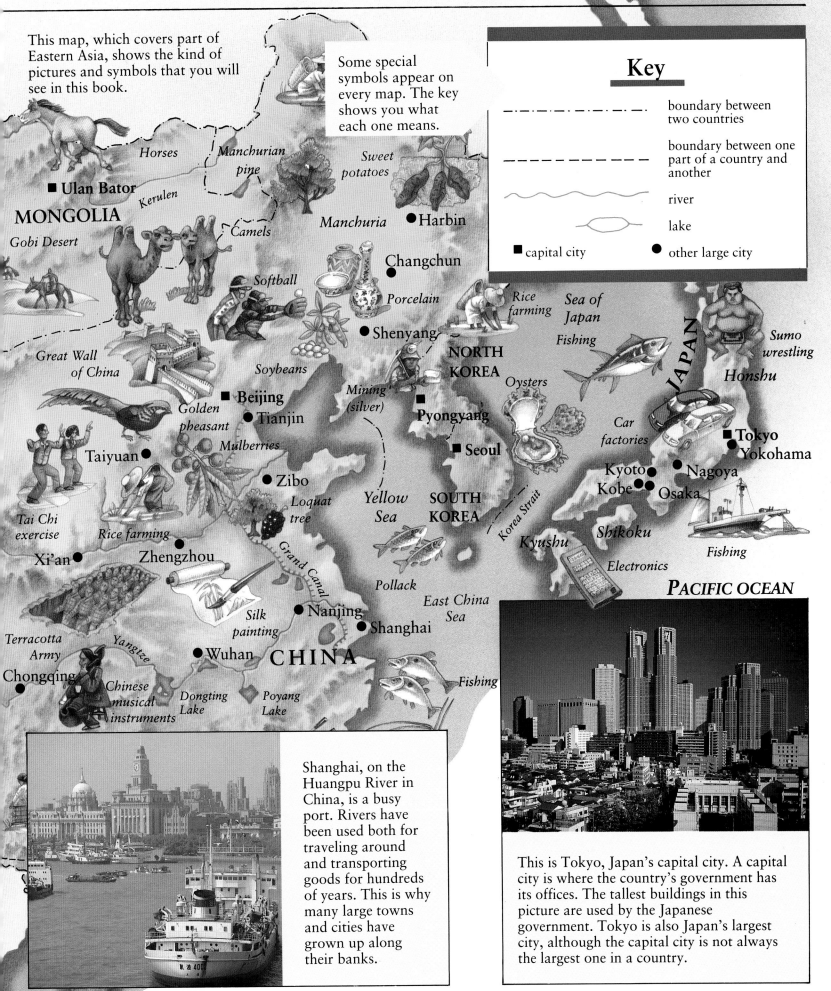

This map, which covers part of Eastern Asia, shows the kind of pictures and symbols that you will see in this book.

Some special symbols appear on every map. The key shows you what each one means.

Key

- ·-·-·-·-·- boundary between two countries
- - - - - - - boundary between one part of a country and another
- ～～～ river
- ◯ lake
- ■ capital city
- ● other large city

Horses

Manchurian pine

Sweet potatoes

■ Ulan Bator

Kerulen

MONGOLIA

Gobi Desert

Camels

Manchuria

● Harbin

● Changchun

Softball

Porcelain

Rice farming

Sea of Japan

Fishing

Shenyang

NORTH KOREA

Oysters

JAPAN

Sumo wrestling

Honshu

Great Wall of China

Soybeans

Mining (silver)

Pyongyang

Car factories

Golden pheasant

■ Beijing

● Tianjin

■ Seoul

● Tokyo

Yokohama

Taiyuan ●

Mulberries

● Zibo

Yellow Sea

SOUTH KOREA

Kyoto ●

Kobe ●

● Nagoya

Osaka

Tai Chi exercise

Rice farming

Loquat tree

Korea Strait

Shikoku

Fishing

Xi'an ●

Zhengzhou ●

Grand Canal

Kyushu

Electronics

PACIFIC OCEAN

Pollack

East China Sea

Silk painting

● Nanjing

● Shanghai

Terracotta Army

Yangtze

● Wuhan

CHINA

Chongqing ●

Chinese musical instruments

Dongting Lake

Poyang Lake

Fishing

Shanghai, on the Huangpu River in China, is a busy port. Rivers have been used both for traveling around and transporting goods for hundreds of years. This is why many large towns and cities have grown up along their banks.

This is Tokyo, Japan's capital city. A capital city is where the country's government has its offices. The tallest buildings in this picture are used by the Japanese government. Tokyo is also Japan's largest city, although the capital city is not always the largest one in a country.

COUNTRIES
OF THE WORLD

People have divided the continents into more than 170 different countries. Each one has its own government and flag. You can see all the flags at the beginning and end of the book. Some countries are so small they are shown on the map only by a number. Look at the list of numbers to find their names. Antarctica is not shown at all because no one lives there and no country rules it.

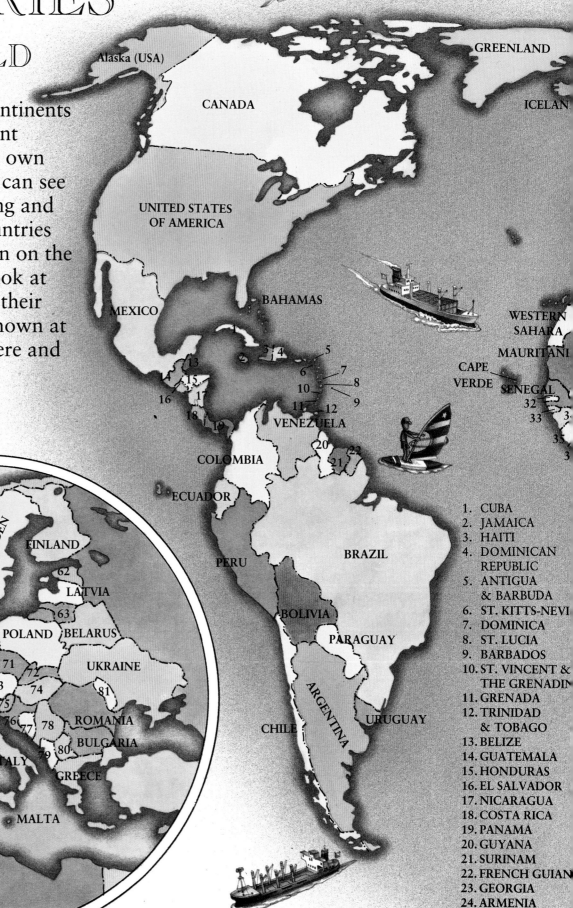

1. CUBA
2. JAMAICA
3. HAITI
4. DOMINICAN REPUBLIC
5. ANTIGUA & BARBUDA
6. ST. KITTS-NEVI
7. DOMINICA
8. ST. LUCIA
9. BARBADOS
10. ST. VINCENT & THE GRENADIN
11. GRENADA
12. TRINIDAD & TOBAGO
13. BELIZE
14. GUATEMALA
15. HONDURAS
16. EL SALVADOR
17. NICARAGUA
18. COSTA RICA
19. PANAMA
20. GUYANA
21. SURINAM
22. FRENCH GUIAN
23. GEORGIA
24. ARMENIA
25. AZERBAIJAN

10

THE RUSSIAN FEDERATION

The Pacific Ocean is too large to include on this map so these island groups are not shown:

Kiribati
Nauru
Tonga
Tuvalu
Western Samoa
Vanuatu
Fiji
Solomon Islands

is area is enlarged on opposite page to ke it easier to read.

6. TUNISIA
7 CYPRUS
8 SYRIA
9 LEBANON
0. ISRAEL
1. JORDAN
2. GAMBIA
3. GUINEA-BISSAU
4. GUINEA
5. SIERRA LEONE
6. LIBERIA
7. IVORY COAST
8. BURKINA FASO
9. GHANA
0. TOGO
1. BENIN

42. SÃO TOMÉ & PRINCIPE
43. EQUATORIAL GUINEA
44. DJIBOUTI
45. UGANDA
46. RWANDA
47. BURUNDI
48. MALAWI
49. SWAZILAND
50. LESOTHO
51. KUWAIT
52. BAHRAIN

53. QATAR
54. UNITED ARAB EMIRATES
55. KYRGYSTAN
56. TADZHIKISTAN
57. BHUTAN
58. BANGLADESH
59. LAOS
60. CAMBODIA (KAMPUCHEA)
61. SINGAPORE
62. ESTONIA
63. LITHUANIA

64. THE NETHERLANDS
65. BELGIUM
66. LUXEMBOURG
67. ANDORRA
68. SWITZERLAND
69. MONACO
70. LIECHTENSTEIN
71. THE CZECH REPUBLIC
72. SLOVAKIA
73. AUSTRIA
74. HUNGARY
75. SLOVENIA
76. CROATIA
77. BOSNIA-HERZEGOVINA
78. YUGOSLAVIA
79. ALBANIA
80. MACEDONIA
81. MOLDOVA
82. SAN MARINO
83. VATICAN CITY

11

WESTERN EUROPE

Most of Western Europe has mild weather, although the far north of Scotland can be bitterly cold in winter, whereas Italy and Spain have very hot summers. There are no deserts in this part of the world. The eight countries packed into this small area all have a large number of towns and cities, lots of industry, and many roads, railways and airports to make traveling around easy.

FACT · FINDER

The HIGHEST MOUNTAIN in Western Europe is Mont Blanc in France. It is 4,807 meters high.

Over 20 MILLION Volkswagen "Beetles" have been made since production first started in Germany in 1938.

Solero de Jerez is the FASTEST FLAMENCO DANCER on record. He can tap his heels 16 times per second.

The LONGEST ROAD TUNNEL in the world is the St. Gotthard tunnel in Switzerland. It is 16.32 km long.

POLAND

Destruction of Berlin wall

Dresden

China

THE CZECH REPUBLIC

Hogs

Berlin

GERMANY

Stein of beer

Mercedes-Benz cars

Hamburg

DENMARK

Frankfurters

Cologne Cathedral

Castles

Windmill

THE NETHERLANDS

Amsterdam

Rotterdam

Bonn

Cod

Luxury chocolates

Brussels

BELGIUM

Lille

Mining (iron ore)

Oil and natural gas

Puffin

NORTH SEA

Cross-channel ferry

Eiffel Tower

Salmon

Golf

Edinburgh

Edinburgh castle

Wedgewood china

UNITED KINGDOM

London

Houses of Parliament

Cricket

Shakespeare

Dairy cattle

Tossing the caber

Ben Nevis

Glasgow

Scotch whisky

Horse jumping

Rugby

Stonehenge

Salmon

Gannet

Giant's Causeway

Irish whisky

Belfast

REPUBLIC OF IRELAND

Dublin

Horse racing

Lobster

Potatoes

ATLANTIC OCEAN

N

E

W

AN	ANDORRA
LI	LIECHTENSTEIN
LX	LUXEMBOURG
MN	MONACO
SM	SAN MARINO
VC	VATICAN CITY

CROATIA

AUSTRIA

Vienna State Opera

SLOVENIA

Snowboarding

Tourism

Zurich

Bern

LI

SWITZERLAND

Mont Blanc

Alps

Skiing

Fashion shoes

Artichokes

Milan

Turin

Pasta

MN

ADRIATIC SEA

Gondolas of Venice

Olive tree

Leaning tower of Pisa

SM

St. Peter's

VC Rome

ITALY

Scuba diving

The Colosseum

Naples

Citrus fruits

Grapes

Sardines

Oil

Mount Etna

Sicily

Corsica

Sardinia

Sheep

Cruising

MEDITERRANEAN SEA

Nuclear power

Famous artists

FRANCE

Lyons

Cannes film festival

Marseilles

Wild horses of the Camargue

Sailing

Anchovies

Waterskiing

Tourism

Minorca

Majorca

Balearic Islands

Wind surfing

Ibiza

Tourism

Paella

Barcelona

AN

Pyrenees

Bicycle racing

Church of Sagrada Família

SPAIN

Wine

Citrus fruits

Wine

Flamenco dancing

The Alhambra

Madrid

El Escorial

Tuna

Strait of Gibraltar

Cork bark

Bull rings

Olive tree

Tower of Belém

Tagus

Lisbon

PORTUGAL

Porto

Port

Mussels

Fishing

Wine

French cheeses

Fast trains

A Pied Piper leads a plague of "rats" through today's Hamelin.

0	150		300 miles	
0	200	400 km		

Harvesting is hard work for both people and animals.

Watery ways

No cars can get into the center of Venice in Italy. You have to walk along winding alleys to see the beautiful old buildings. Or, better still, you can take a gondola along the canals as people have done for many hundreds of years.

EASTERN EUROPE

Mountains cover most of Eastern Europe except in Poland and Hungary. The Danube River flows through flat farmland across Hungary and Yugoslavia and between Romania and Bulgaria. The winters are cold in the north and in the mountains. Summer is hot, especially in the south. Many tourists come to Greece to enjoy the sunshine.

Best dresses

Two Polish girls dressed up for a special occasion. They are wearing the national costume for their region. Poland has many national costumes because many different groups of people live within its borders.

N
W — E
S

Baltic Sea

Sunbathing

Tourism

Shipbuilding

Gdansk

Flax

Striped field mouse

Traditional farming

European bison

Birch tree

Wisła

POLAND

● Lodz

Potatoes

Pigs

Mining (copper)

Skiing

Warsaw

Outdoor cafés

Wheat

Flower market

Skiing

● Krakow

Open-air Catholic service

Walking and biking

Chamois goat

UKRAINE

Wolf

Carpathian Mountains

Pine forests

Prut

MOLDOVA

Bran Castle

Wild boar

ROMANIA

Factories

Folk dancing

GERMANY

Charles Bridge

Bohemian crystal

Prague

CZECH REPUBLIC

Beer

Factories

Church in Brno

Wooden houses

Car factory

AUSTRIA

Bratislava

SLOVAKIA

Wine

Slav wedding

Tisza

Budapest

HUNGARY

Sailing on Lake Balaton

European hamster

Geese

Paddle steamer on Danube

SLOVENIA

Ljubljana

CROATIA

Zagreb

Sunflowers

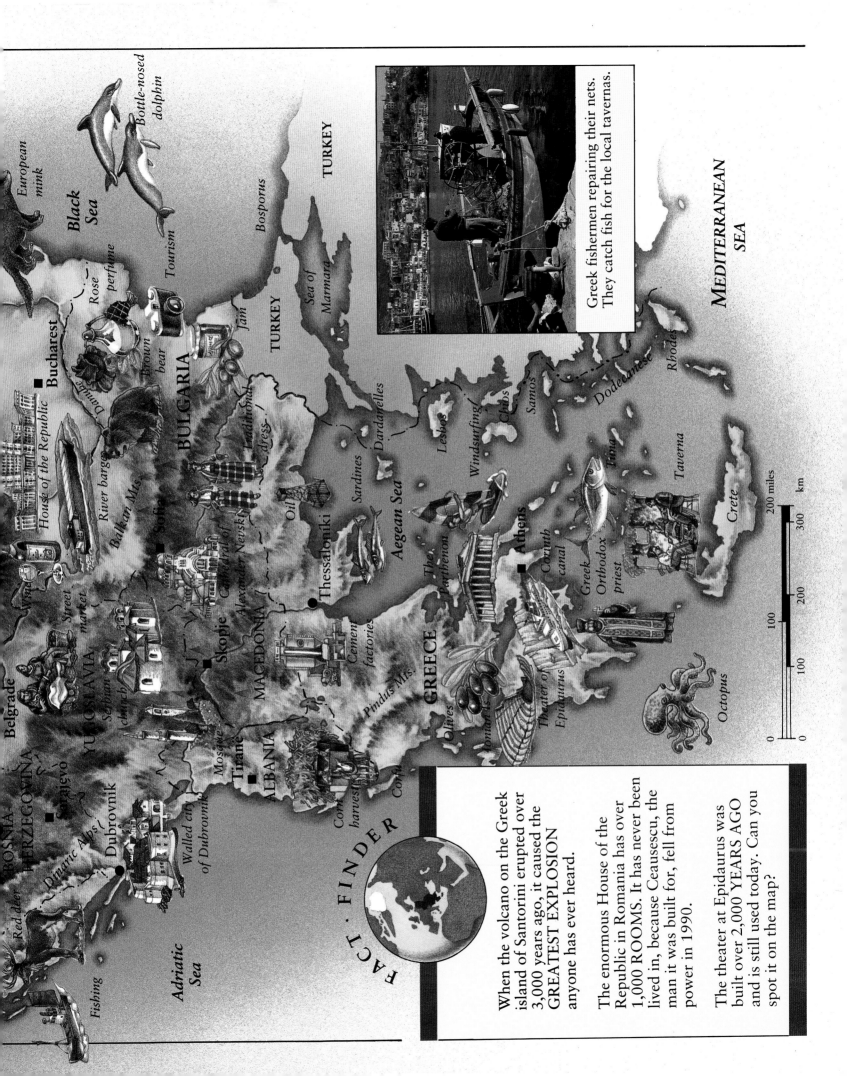

Greek fishermen repairing their nets. They catch fish for the local tavernas.

FACT FINDER

When the volcano on the Greek island of Santorini erupted over 3,000 years ago, it caused the GREATEST EXPLOSION anyone has ever heard.

The enormous House of the Republic in Romania has over 1,000 ROOMS. It has never been lived in, because Ceausescu, the man it was built for, fell from power in 1990.

The theater at Epidaurus was built over 2,000 YEARS AGO and is still used today. Can you spot it on the map?

SCANDINAVIA

The five countries of Northern Europe all lie near the North Pole, so they all have the same kind of weather – short summers and long, freezing winters. Very few people live in the far north of Norway, Sweden and Finland, where snow covers the ground for much of the year. Most of the population live in the warmer south, where the land is green with forests and farmland.

Colorful in the Cold

Lapland lies in the far north of Norway, Sweden and Finland. The people who live there are called Lapps. They wear colorful woollen clothes and reindeer-skin boots to keep them warm in the icy winters.

THE RUSSIAN FEDERATION

Arctic Circle

Ski jumping

Hydroelectric power

Wolves

Kemi

Salmon

Northern lights

Lake Inari

Midnight sun

Reindeer herding

L a p l a n d

Lapp crafts

Forestry

Forestry

North Cape

ARCTIC OCEAN

Muonio

Lapp woman

Mining (iron)

Lulea

Wolverine

Hydroelectric power

Fishing trawler

N
E
S
W

Elk

Arctic Circle

Reindeer

Lemming

Fishing trawler

Lofoten Islands

Maelstrom whirlpool

Hydroelectric power

Forestry

ICELAND

Midnight sun

Glacier

Cod

Vatnajokull

Volcano

Geyser

Reykjavik

Fishing trawler

Although Iceland is often very cold, the people who live there can swim outdoors in hot springs at most times in the year. The water is heated by red-hot lava which seeps up through cracks in the earth in many parts of the country.

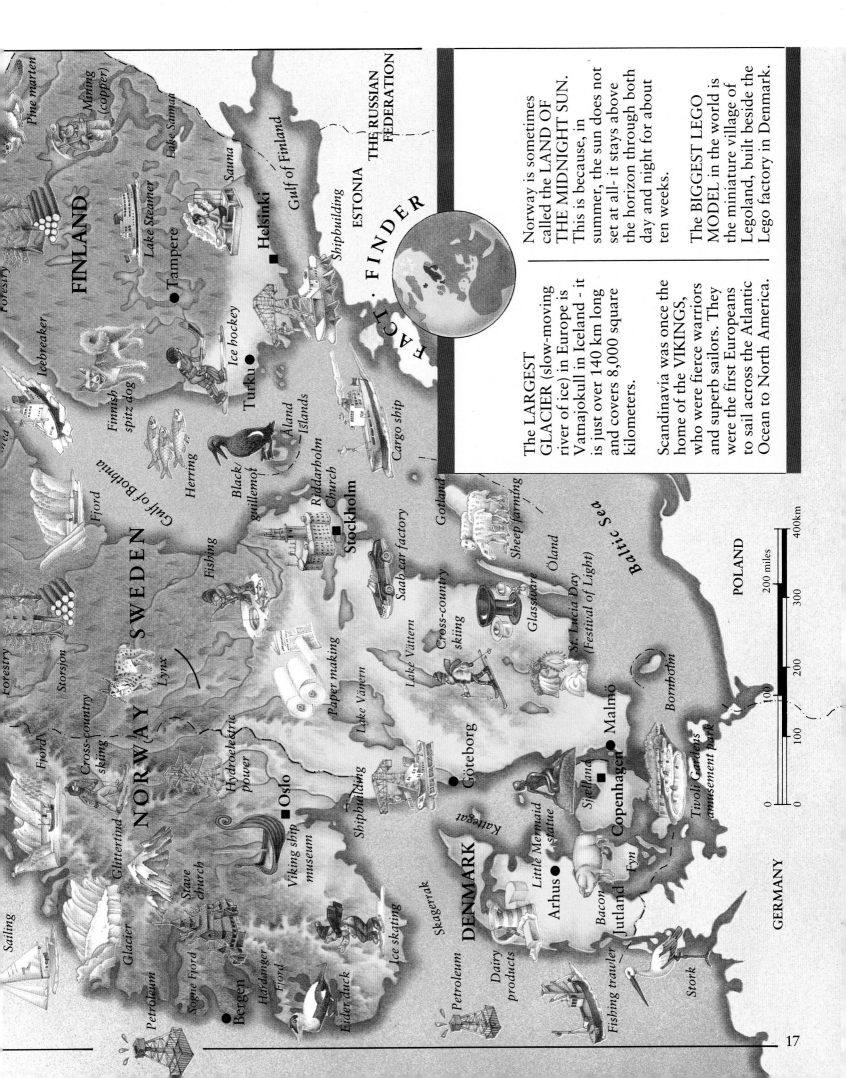

FINLAND

Pine marten

Mining (copper)

Forestry

Lake Saimaa

Lake Steamer

Tampere

Icebreaker

Sauna

Finnish spitz dog

Herring

Helsinki

Turku

Gulf of Finland

Black guillemot

Åland Islands

Ice hockey

Shipbuilding

ESTONIA

THE RUSSIAN FEDERATION

Cargo ship

FACT · FINDER

Riddarholm Church

Stockholm

Saab car factory

Gotland

Sheep farming

Öland

The LARGEST GLACIER (slow-moving river of ice) in Europe is Vatnajokull in Iceland - it is just over 140 km long and covers 8,000 square kilometers.

Scandinavia was once the home of the VIKINGS, who were fierce warriors and superb sailors. They were the first Europeans to sail across the Atlantic Ocean to North America.

Norway is sometimes called the LAND OF THE MIDNIGHT SUN. This is because, in summer, the sun does not set at all - it stays above the horizon through both day and night for about ten weeks.

The BIGGEST LEGO MODEL in the world is the miniature village of Legoland, built beside the Lego factory in Denmark.

SWEDEN

Fjord

Gulf of Bothnia

Fishing

NORWAY

Forestry

Storsjon

Lynx

Cross-country skiing

Fjord

Glittertind

Glacier

Hydroelectric power

Paper making

Lake Vänern

Lake Vättern

Cross-country skiing

Glassware

St. Lucia Day (Festival of Light)

Baltic Sea

Bornholm

POLAND

0   100   200   300   400km

0   100   200 miles

Petroleum

Sogne Fjord

Bergen

Hardanger Fjord

Stave church

Sailing

Eider duck

Viking ship museum

Oslo

Shipbuilding

Ice skating

Skagerrak

Göteborg

Kattegat

Little Mermaid statue

Sjælland

Malmö

Copenhagen

Tivoli Gardens amusement park

DENMARK

Arhus

Bacon

Jutland

Fyn

Petroleum

Dairy products

Fishing trawler

Stork

GERMANY

17

RUSSIA AND THE NEW INDEPENDENT STATES

The Ural Mountains divide the Russian Federation into two parts. Most cities and farms are west and south of the Urals and most people live there. Siberia to the east is cold and bleak. A huge forest of fir and pine trees covers much of the north. South of it lies a vast, grassy plain called the steppes.

FACT · FINDER

The Russian Federation is the LARGEST COUNTRY in the world. It is nearly twice as big as Canada, the second largest.

Russia is so WIDE it takes 7 days to travel across it on the Trans-Siberian railway.

REINDEERS really do pull sleds in the cold, snowy lands of the far north.

Lake Baikal is the world's DEEPEST lake. You could sink five Empire State buildings in it, one on top of the other.

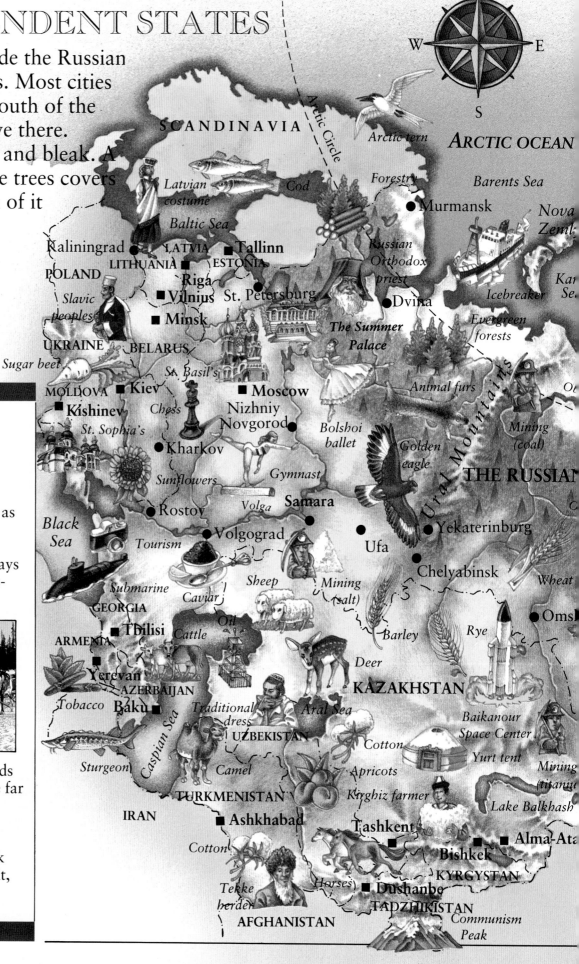

N
W · E
S

SCANDINAVIA

Arctic Circle

Arctic tern

ARCTIC OCEAN

Forestry

Barents Sea

Cod

● Murmansk

Nova Zeml

Latvian costume

Baltic Sea

Russian Orthodox priest

Icebreaker

Kar Se

Kaliningrad ■

LATVIA

■ Tallinn

ESTONIA

LITHUANIA

St. Petersburg

● Dvina

Evergreen forests

POLAND

■ Riga

■ Vilnius

Slavic peoples

■ Minsk

The Summer Palace

UKRAINE

BELARUS

Sugar beet

St. Basil's

Animal furs

MOLDOVA

● Kiev

■ Moscow

Mining (coal)

● Kishinev

Chess

Nizhniy Novgorod ●

Bolshoi ballet

St. Sophia's

Golden eagle

Ural Mountains

THE RUSSIAN

● Kharkov

Gymnast

Sunflowers

Volga

● Samara

● Rostov

Volgograd ●

● Yekaterinburg

Black Sea

Tourism

● Ufa

Wheat

Submarine

Sheep

Mining (salt)

Chelyabinsk

● Oms

Caviar

Barley

Rye

GEORGIA

■ Tbilisi

Cattle

Oil

Deer

KAZAKHSTAN

ARMENIA

● Yerevan

AZERBAIJAN

● Baku ■

Traditional dress

Aral Sea

Baikanour Space Center

Tobacco

Cotton

Yurt tent

Mining (titaniu

Sturgeon

Caspian Sea

UZBEKISTAN

Camel

Apricots

Lake Balkhash

TURKMENISTAN

Kirghiz farmer

IRAN

■ Ashkhabad

Tashkent

● Alma-Ata

Cotton

Bishkek ■

KYRGYSTAN

Tekke herder

Horses

● Dushanbe

TADZHIKISTAN

AFGHANISTAN

Communism Peak

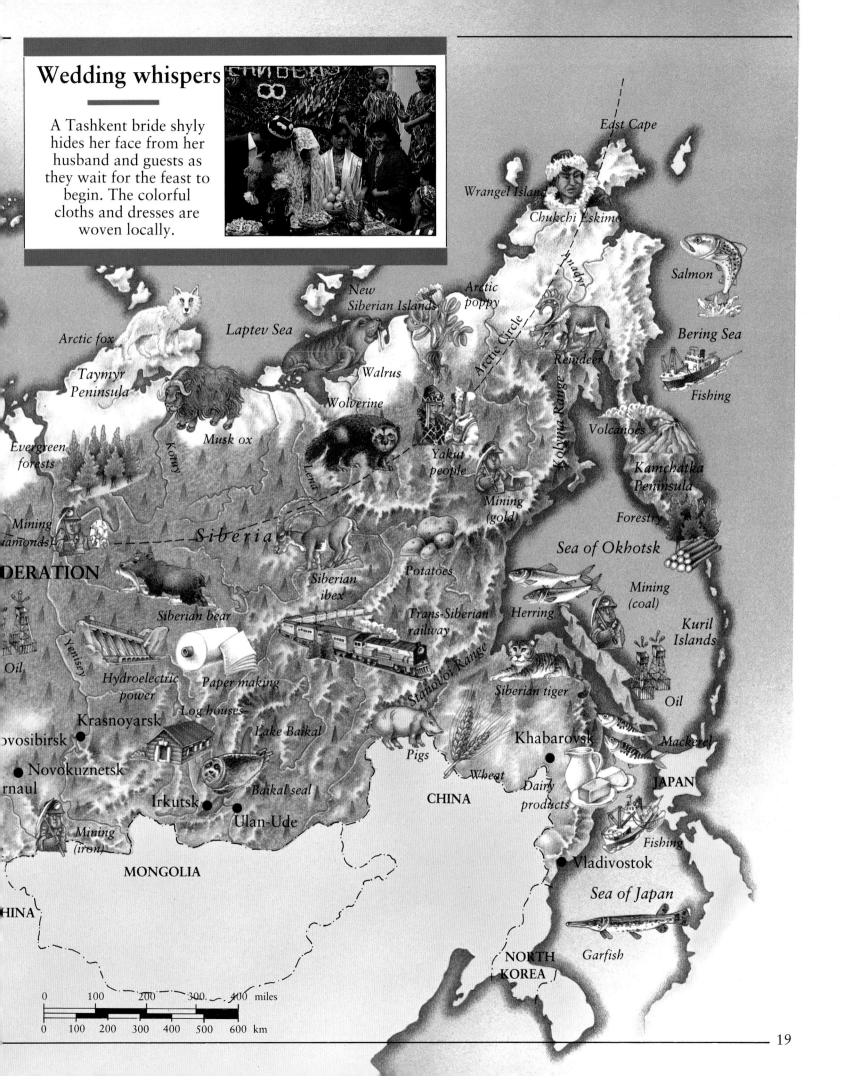

Wedding whispers

A Tashkent bride shyly hides her face from her husband and guests as they wait for the feast to begin. The colorful cloths and dresses are woven locally.

East Cape

Wrangel Island

Chukchi Eskimo

Salmon

New Siberian Islands

Arctic poppy

Laptev Sea

Arctic Circle

Bering Sea

Arctic fox

Walrus

Reindeer

Fishing

Taymyr Peninsula

Wolverine

Volcanoes

Musk ox

Kotuy

Yakut people

Kamchatka Peninsula

Evergreen forests

Lena

Mining (gold)

Forestry

Mining (diamonds)

Siberia

Sea of Okhotsk

DERATION

Potatoes

Siberian ibex

Mining (coal)

Trans-Siberian railway

Herring

Kuril Islands

Siberian bear

Yenisey

Oil

Stanovoi Range

Siberian tiger

Oil

Hydroelectric power

Paper making

Log houses

Krasnoyarsk

Khabarovsk

Mackerel

Lake Baikal

Pigs

Novosibirsk

Wheat

JAPAN

Novokuznetsk

Baikal seal

Dairy products

rnaul

Irkutsk

CHINA

Ulan-Ude

Mining (iron)

Vladivostok

MONGOLIA

Sea of Japan

HINA

NORTH KOREA

Garfish

| 0 | 100 | 200 | 300 | 400 miles |

| 0 | 100 | 200 | 300 | 400 | 500 | 600 km |

19

THE MIDDLE EAST

Much of the Middle East has hot, dry weather for most of the year. There are hundreds of miles of sandy desert, where very little can survive in the blistering heat. Huge oil fields lie underneath some of these deserts and under the waters of the Gulf. Countries like Saudi Arabia and Qatar have become very rich by pumping the oil from the ground and selling it to other countries all over the world.

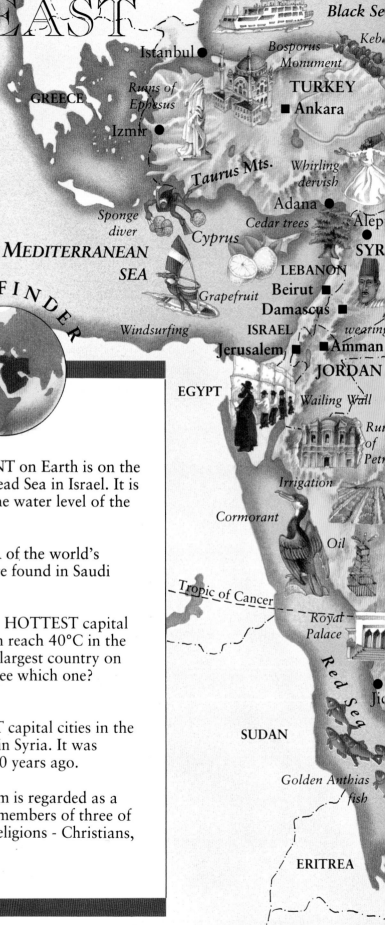

BULGARIA
Ferry
Black Se
Istanbul
Bosporus
Monument
Keb
Ruins of
Ephesus
TURKEY
GREECE
Ankara
Izmir
Taurus Mts.
Whirling
dervish
Adana
Alep
Sponge
diver
Cyprus
Cedar trees
SYR
MEDITERRANEAN
SEA
Grapefruit
LEBANON
Beirut
Damascus
Windsurfing
ISRAEL
wearin
Jerusalem
Amman
JORDAN
EGYPT
Wailing Wall
Rui
of
Petr
Irrigation
Cormorant
Oil
Tropic of Cancer
Royal
Palace
Red Sea
SUDAN
Golden Anthias
fish
ERITREA
ETHIOPIA

A Syrian girl steals a kiss from her new sister.

Look, no hands - floating is easy on the salty Dead Sea.

FACT · FINDER

The LOWEST POINT on Earth is on the shore of the salty Dead Sea in Israel. It is 399 meters below the water level of the world's oceans.

About a QUARTER of the world's entire oil reserves are found in Saudi Arabia.

Temperatures in the HOTTEST capital city in the world can reach 40°C in the summer. It is in the largest country on this map. Can you see which one? (Answer: page 48)

One of the OLDEST capital cities in the world is Damascus in Syria. It was founded about 5,000 years ago.

The city of Jerusalem is regarded as a HOLY PLACE for members of three of the world's major religions - Christians, Muslims and Jews.

THE RUSSIAN FEDERATION

KAZAKHSTAN

GEORGIA

ARMENIA

Cotton
AZERBAIJAN

Caspian Sea

TURKMENISTAN

Lake Van

● Tabriz

Lake Urmia

Sturgeon

Elburz Mts.

Meshed ●

N
W   E
S

Wanderers

Some people of the Middle East, called nomads, live in tents. They travel around from place to place, taking their herds of camels, sheep or goats with them.

Muslims

*...tages of
...d huts*

*Corkscrew-shaped
tower*

Teheran ■

Royal Mosque

Persian carpets

Euphrates

*Traditional
dress*

Baghdad ■

Tigris

Zagros Mts.

IRAN

● Isfahan

*Wandering
peoples*

Shepherds

IRAQ

*Oil
tanker*

KUWAIT

Kuwait ■

Oil rig

● Shiraz

*Ruins of
Persepolis*

Onager

*Natural
gas*

*Desert
locusts*

PAKISTAN

Frankincense

*...ian
...ert*

Goats

*Racing
camels*

*Oil
sheikh*

The Gulf

Oil

Oil

Gulf of Oman

Tropic of Cancer

ARABIAN SEA

Horses

Manama ■

QATAR

BAHRAIN

■ Doha

Riyadh ■

*Street
market*

■ Abu Dhabi

Muscat ■

*Date
palm*

Oysters

UNITED ARAB
EMIRATES

SAUDI ARABIA

*Arabian
oryx*

Swamp

*Traditional
headdress*

Oil

...ecca

*Bedouin
people*

*Desert
landscape*

OMAN

*Desalination
plant*

Rub'al Khali

Camels

Kuria Muria Islands

*Buildings
in San'a*

Goatherds

*Washing clothes
in stream*

Falcon

■ San'a

YEMEN

*Yemen coin
showing
coffee plant*

Oil

Gulf of Aden

Sardines

Arab dhow

Socotra

Aden ●

The whole family help out during the cotton-picking season in Turkey.

0		250		500 miles

0	250	500	750 km

21

SOUTH ASIA

South Asia is one of the world's most crowded places. It is usually hot and humid but has a very rainy season called the monsoon. It is home to many wild creatures, such as tigers and elephants, and has the world's highest mountain, Mount Everest, in the Himalayas.

The HIGHEST MOUNTAIN in the world is Mount Everest on the Nepal-Tibet border in the Himalayas. It is 8,848 meters high. The Himalaya-Karakoram range has 96 peaks that are over 7,300 meters.

One of the most BEAUTIFUL BUILDINGS in the world is the tomb known as the Taj Mahal. It was built by a ruler of India in memory of his favorite wife. It took 20,000 workers 20 years to build it.

The Ganges is one of the LONGEST RIVERS in the world. It starts in an ice cave, over 3,000 meters up in the Himalaya mountains. Can you see where it ends? (Answer: page 48)

DANGEROUS ANIMALS! People who live outside the towns sometimes have to worry about such creatures as crocodiles, leopards, rhinoceroses, scorpions, tigers, and poisonous snakes.

Fathers in Bhutan often carry their children around on their backs like this.

A snake has no ears, so it cannot hear. It is the rhythmic, swaying movements of the charmer, not the music of his flute, that makes the snake raise its head and neck from the basket to watch.

N E S W

CHINA

TURKMENISTAN

UZBEKISTAN

TADZHIKISTAN

IRAN

Wheat

Camel transport

Blue mosque

Kabul

Mining
(Lapis lazuli)

AFGHANISTAN

Hindu Kush

Khyber Pass

Muslim at prayer

Islamabad

Lahore

Kashmir

Mount Godwin Austen

Woman wearing sari

HIMALAYAS

Street

Irrigation

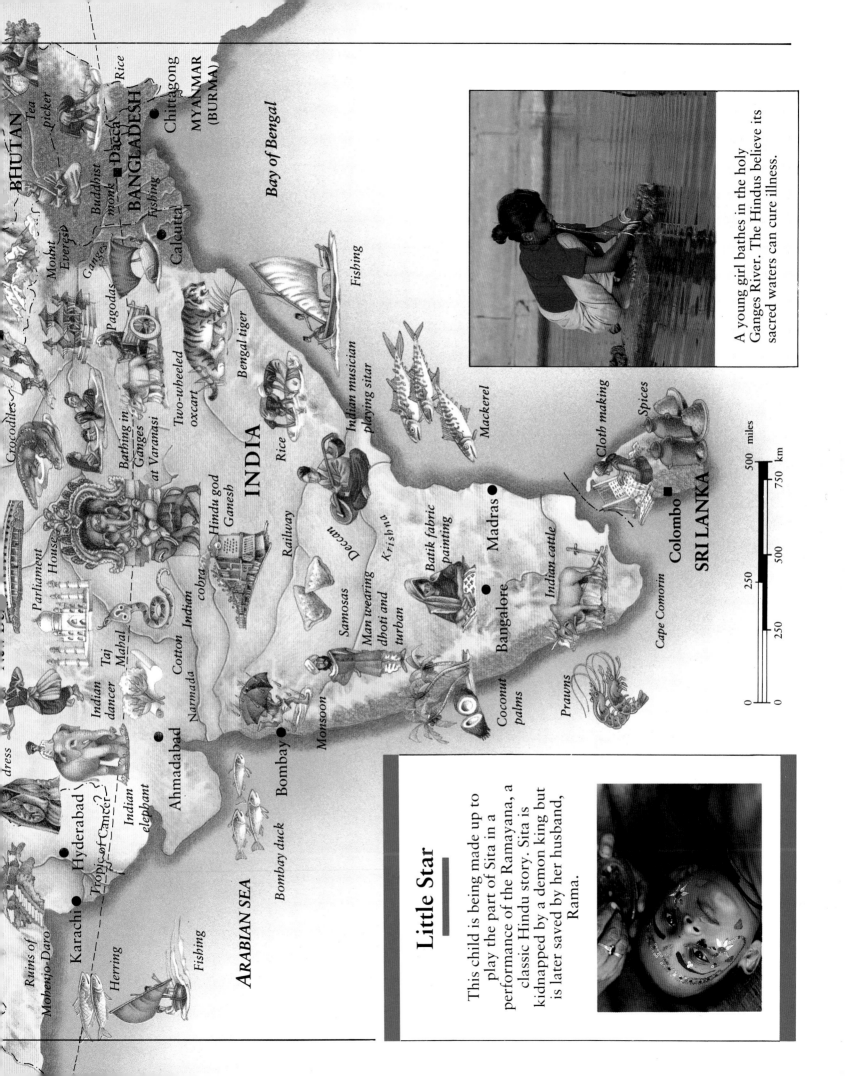

A young girl bathes in the holy Ganges River. The Hindus believe its sacred waters can cure illness.

Little Star

This child is being made up to play the part of Sita in a performance of the Ramayana, a classic Hindu story. Sita is kidnapped by a demon king but is later saved by her husband, Rama.

EASTERN ASIA

Eastern Asia has many different kinds of landscapes including high mountains, like those in Tibet, and hot deserts, such as the Gobi, as well as huge plains where farmers grow rice, tea and other crops. China is by far the largest country in this area. Japan is made up of a group of islands - 4 main ones and about 3,000 much smaller ones.

KAZAKHSTAN

Altai Mountains

Selenga

Nomadic herders

Sheep

Dzungarian Desert

Mining (coal)

Goats

MONGOLIA

Tea picking

Tian Shan

Turpan Depression

CHINA

TADZHIKISTAN

Musk deer

Taklimakan Desert

Yak

Monsoon

Giant panda

Przewalski horse

Kunlun Mountains

Red panda

Yak

Mining (salt)

Musk perfume

Pagoda

Oil

Plateau of Tibet

Buddhist monk

Carpet making

Tibetan terrier

Bicycles

Chengd

INDIA

Potala Palace

Himalaya Mountains

Barley

Yalong

NEPAL

BHUTAN

Bambo

Lychees

Tropic of Cancer

Mekong

MYANMAR (BURMA)

LAOS

N W E S

Keep out!

A school trip visits the Great Wall of China. The wall, which is over 6,000 km long, was built more than 2,000 years ago to protect China from enemies.

Mount Fuji, the highest peak in Japan, was once an active volcano.

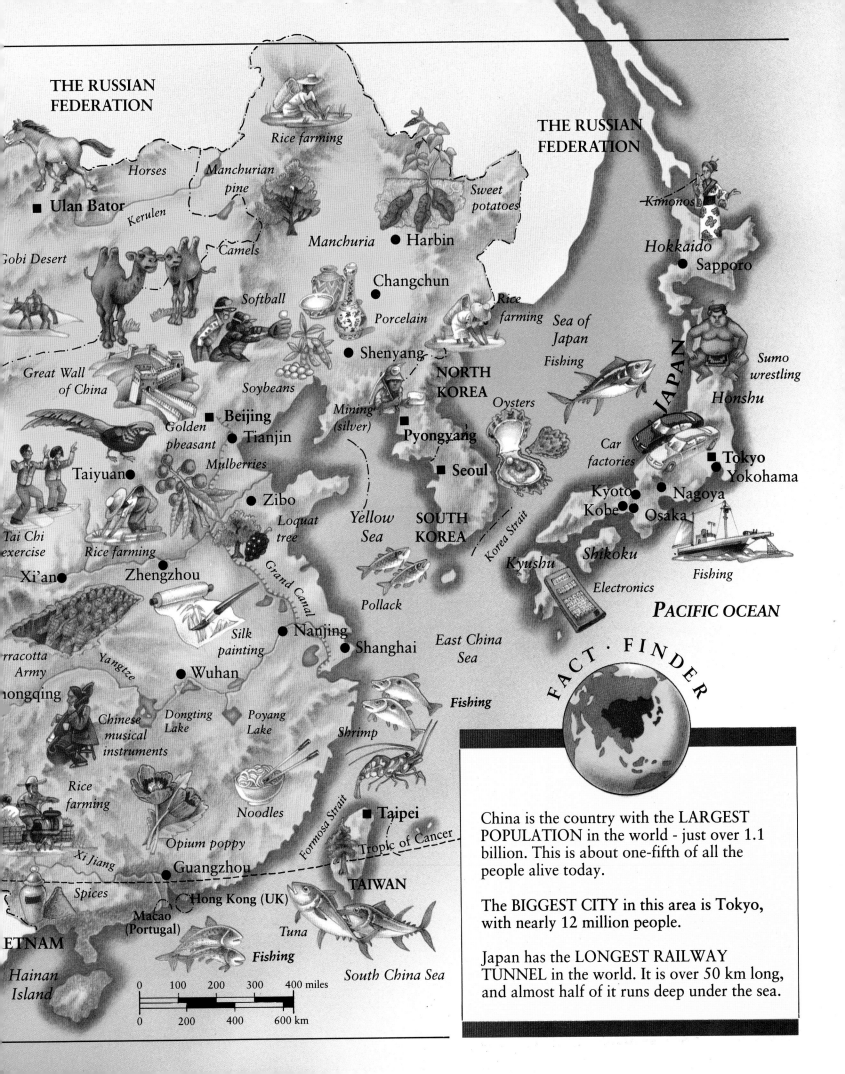

THE RUSSIAN
FEDERATION

Rice farming

Horses
*Manchurian
pine*

*Sweet
potatoes*

THE RUSSIAN
FEDERATION

■ **Ulan Bator**

Kerulen

Manchuria ● **Harbin**

Kimonos

Camels

Gobi Desert

Hokkaido
● **Sapporo**

● **Changchun**

Softball

Porcelain

*Rice
farming*

*Sea of
Japan*

*Sumo
wrestling*

Fishing

JAPAN

Honshu

*Great Wall
of China*

● **Shenyang**

Soybeans

**NORTH
KOREA**

Oysters

*Car
factories*

*Mining
(silver)*

Beijing ■

*Golden
pheasant*

● **Tianjin**

Pyongyang ■

Mulberries

Kyoto ● **Tokyo** ■
● *Yokohama*

Taiyuan ●

■ **Seoul**

● **Nagoya**

Kobe ● *Osaka*

*Tai Chi
exercise*

● **Zibo**

*Loquat
tree*

*Yellow
Sea*

**SOUTH
KOREA**

Korea Strait

Shikoku

Kyushu

Fishing

Xi'an ●

Rice farming

● **Zhengzhou**

Grand Canal

Pollack

Electronics

PACIFIC OCEAN

*Terracotta
Army*

Yangtze

*Silk
painting*

● **Nanjing**

*East China
Sea*

F A C T · F I N D E R

hongqing

● **Wuhan**

● **Shanghai**

*Chinese
musical
instruments*

*Dongting
Lake*

*Poyang
Lake*

Fishing

Shrimp

*Rice
farming*

Noodles

Opium poppy

Tropic of Cancer

Taipei ■

China is the country with the LARGEST
POPULATION in the world - just over 1.1
billion. This is about one-fifth of all the
people alive today.

Xi Jiang

● **Guangzhou**

Formosa Strait

TAIWAN

The BIGGEST CITY in this area is Tokyo,
with nearly 12 million people.

Spices

Hong Kong (UK)

*Macao
(Portugal)*

Tuna

ETNAM

*Hainan
Island*

Fishing

South China Sea

Japan has the LONGEST RAILWAY
TUNNEL in the world. It is over 50 km long,
and almost half of it runs deep under the sea.

| 0 | 100 | 200 | 300 | 400 miles |

| 0 | 200 | 400 | 600 km |

SOUTHEAST ASIA

Southeast Asia is very hot and often very wet. The tropical rain forests are being cleared for farmland and fast-growing towns. But there are some National Parks where trees and wildlife are protected. Some mountains are volcanoes: there are 77 active ones in Indonesia! In the Philippines, 250,000 people had to flee from Mount Pinatubo in 1991-92.

CHINA

Forestry

MYANMAR (BURMA)

Irrawaddy

Elephant hauling teak log

LAOS

Cyclists

Hanoi

Rice farming

■ **Vientiane**

Rangoon ■

Chinese junk

N
W E
S

Andaman Islands

Spanish mackerel

Tourism

THAILAND
Bangkok ■

CAMBODIA (KAMPUCHEA)

Angkor Wat

VIETNAM

Floating market

Phnom Penh ■

● **Ho Chi Minh City**

Tourism

Drying fish

Containership

Rubber trees

Shadow Puppets

Puppet shows are popular in Indonesia. Amazing puppets are held up on sticks behind a white screen. The audience sees their shadows in front of a bright light. Perhaps you can make your own shadow-puppet show.

Rubber trees

Medan ■

Oil

Kuala Lumpur ■

MALAYSIA

Skyscrapers

SINGAPORE

Bandar Seri Begawan
BRUNEI ■

Orangut

Rubber trees

Giant flowers

Sumatra

INDIAN OCEAN

Tiger

Coffee

Bangka

Borobudur Temple

INDONESIA

Borneo

■ **Jakarta** ●

Bandung

Semarang ●

Surabaya
Tourism

Java

Bali

Fishing

Batik cloth

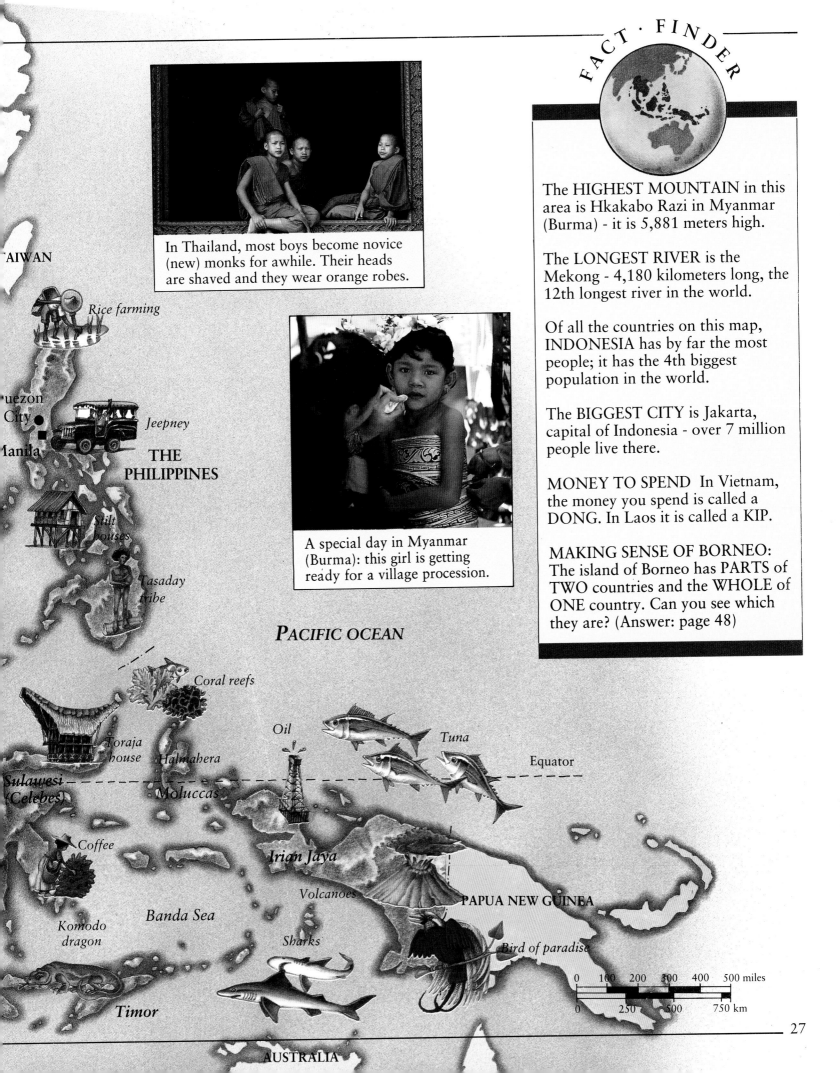

In Thailand, most boys become novice (new) monks for awhile. Their heads are shaved and they wear orange robes.

The HIGHEST MOUNTAIN in this area is Hkakabo Razi in Myanmar (Burma) - it is 5,881 meters high.

The LONGEST RIVER is the Mekong - 4,180 kilometers long, the 12th longest river in the world.

Of all the countries on this map, INDONESIA has by far the most people; it has the 4th biggest population in the world.

The BIGGEST CITY is Jakarta, capital of Indonesia - over 7 million people live there.

MONEY TO SPEND In Vietnam, the money you spend is called a DONG. In Laos it is called a KIP.

MAKING SENSE OF BORNEO: The island of Borneo has PARTS of TWO countries and the WHOLE of ONE country. Can you see which they are? (Answer: page 48)

A special day in Myanmar (Burma): this girl is getting ready for a village procession.

TAIWAN

Rice farming

Quezon City

Manila

Jeepney

THE PHILIPPINES

Stilt houses

Tasaday tribe

PACIFIC OCEAN

Coral reefs

Oil

Tuna

Equator

Toraja house

Halmahera

Sulawesi (Celebes)

Moluccas

Coffee

Irian Jaya

Volcanoes

PAPUA NEW GUINEA

Banda Sea

Komodo dragon

Sharks

Bird of paradise

Timor

| 0 | 100 | 200 | 300 | 400 | 500 miles |

| 0 | 250 | 500 | 750 km |

AUSTRALIA

27

NORTHERN AFRICA

The Sahara Desert covers most of northern Africa. It is scorching hot in the daytime but cold at night. Plants and crops grow around the coast and along the banks of the Nile River. Steamy rain forests once stretched from Sierra Leone to the Cameroon, but most of the trees have been cut down to make room for cocoa, coffee and other crops.

FACT · FINDER

The Sahara Desert is the LARGEST DESERT and it is getting bigger. It spreads at the rate of a football field every 15 seconds.

Massive stone statues guard the ancient temple of Abu Simbel. During the mid-1960s, in an amazing FEAT OF ENGINEERING, the whole structure was moved, piece by piece, up onto higher ground. This was to make way for the huge reservoir now known as Lake Nasser.

FRANC

SPAIN

PORTUGAL

Shrimp

Algiers

Couscous

Rabat ■ ● Fez

Casablanca ●

MOROCCO *Atlas Mountains*

● Marrakesh

Berber women

Scorpion

Addax antelope

Sa ha ra

ALGERI

ATLANTIC OCEAN

Tourism

Canary Islands (Spain)

Las Palmas ●

■ **El Aaiún**

WESTERN SAHARA

Sardines

Camel carava

Tropic of Cancer

Mining (iron)

Jackal

Nomadic herds

Mini (uraniu

Nomad camp

MAURITANIA

Fishing from beach

MALI

Sankore mosque, Timbuktu

■

Nouakchott

SENEGAL

Hyena

Dogon dancer

Slender-snouted crocodile

Ancie Nok civiliza

Dakar ■

Peanuts

GAMBIA

Giraffe

Niamey ■

Banjul ■

GUINEA-BISSAU

■ **Bamako**

BURKINA FASO

Bissau ■

Ouagadougou

Conakry ■

Mud hut village

GHANA

BENIN *Yams*

SIERRA LEONE

GUINEA

Ab

Freetown ■

Lake Volta

TOGO

Dia mon

Pygmy hippopotamus

Porto-Novo ■

Monrovia ■

IVORY COAST

■ ■ ■

Accra ■ **Lome** **Lagos**

LIBERIA

Abidjan

ATLANTIC OCEAN

Tuna

Equator

Lomé cathedral

Shrimp

Oil

0	200	400	600	800	1000 miles

0	400	800	1200	1600 km

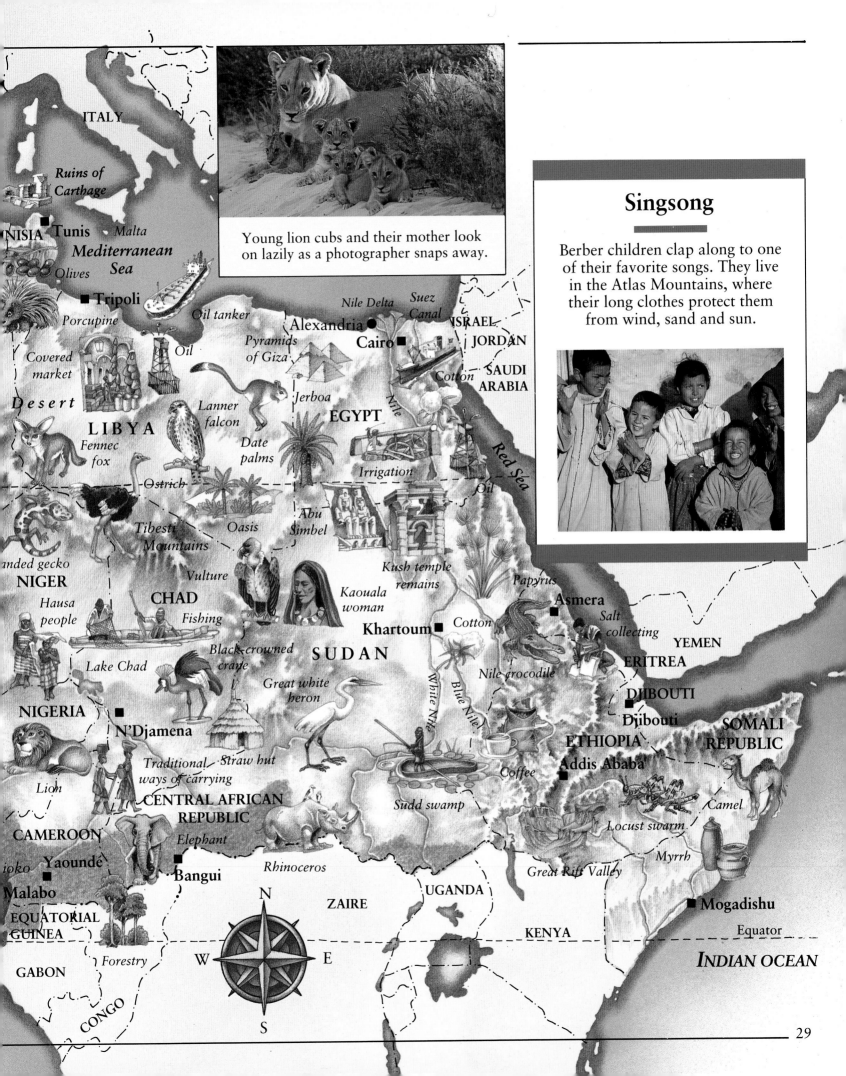

ITALY

Ruins of Carthage

■ **Tunis**
NISIA

Malta

Mediterranean Sea

Olives

Porcupine

■ **Tripoli**

Oil tanker

Young lion cubs and their mother look on lazily as a photographer snaps away.

Singsong

Berber children clap along to one of their favorite songs. They live in the Atlas Mountains, where their long clothes protect them from wind, sand and sun.

Nile Delta

Suez Canal

Alexandria

Pyramids of Giza

●
Cairo ■

ISRAEL

JORDAN

Cotton

SAUDI ARABIA

Covered market

Oil

Desert

Oil

L I B Y A

Fennec fox

Lanner falcon

Jerboa

EGYPT

Date palms

Nile

Red Sea

−Ostrich−

Irrigation

Oil

Tibesti Mountains

Oasis

Abu Simbel

nded gecko

Vulture

Kush temple remains

Papyrus

Asmera ■

Salt collecting

NIGER

Kaouala woman

YEMEN

Hausa people

CHAD

Fishing

Khartoum ■

Cotton

Nile crocodile

ERITREA

Khartoum ■

S U D A N

■ **DJIBOUTI**

Black-crowned crane

Great white heron

White Nile

Blue Nile

Djibouti ■

SOMALI REPUBLIC

Lake Chad

NIGERIA ■

N'Djamena ■

Straw hut

Coffee

ETHIOPIA

Addis Ababa ■

Lion

Traditional ways of carrying

CENTRAL AFRICAN REPUBLIC

Sudd swamp

Locust swarm

Camel

CAMEROON

Elephant

Myrrh

ioko **Yaoundé** ■

Bangui ■

Rhinoceros

Great Rift Valley

Mogadishu ■

Malabo

EQUATORIAL GUINEA

UGANDA

ZAIRE

KENYA

Equator

N

GABON

Forestry

W   E

INDIAN OCEAN

CONGO

S

29

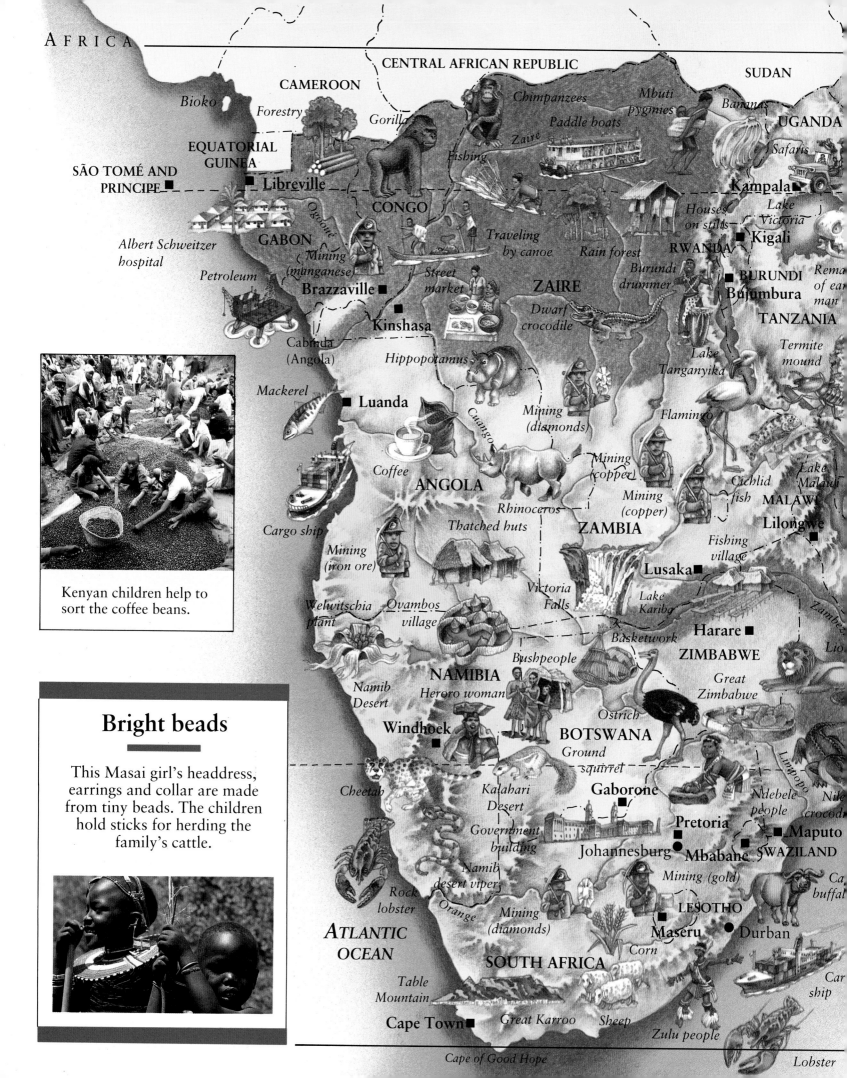

CENTRAL AFRICAN REPUBLIC

CAMEROON

SUDAN

Bioko

Forestry

Gorilla

Chimpanzees

Mbuti pygmies

Bananas

UGANDA

EQUATORIAL GUINEA

Paddle boats

Zaire

Fishing

SÃO TOMÉ AND PRINCIPE

Libreville

Houses on stilts

Kampala

Safaris

CONGO

Traveling by canoe

Rain forest

RWANDA

Lake Victoria

GABON

Ogooué

Mining (manganese)

Street market

Kigali

Albert Schweitzer hospital

ZAIRE

Burundi drummer

BURUNDI

Bujumbura

Rema of ear man

Petroleum

Brazzaville

Dwarf crocodile

TANZANIA

Lake Tanganyika

Kinshasa

Termite mound

Cabinda (Angola)

Hippopotamus

Mackerel

Luanda

Mining (diamonds)

Flamingo

Cuango

Lake Malawi

Coffee

ANGOLA

Mining (copper)

Cichlid fish

MALAWI

Mining (copper)

Lilongwe

Cargo ship

Rhinoceros

ZAMBIA

Fishing village

Mining (iron ore)

Thatched huts

Lusaka

Welwitschia plant

Ovambos village

Victoria Falls

Lake Kariba

Zambe

Basketwork

Harare

Bushpeople

ZIMBABWE

Lio

NAMIBIA

Great Zimbabwe

Heroro woman

Ostrich

Namib Desert

Ground squirrel

Windhoek

BOTSWANA

Limpopo

Cheetah

Ndebele people

Nile crocod

Kalahari Desert

Gaborone

Government building

Pretoria

Maputo

Namib desert viper

Johannesburg

Mbabane

SWAZILAND

Rock lobster

Mining (gold)

Ca buffal

Orange

Mining (diamonds)

LESOTHO

ATLANTIC OCEAN

Corn

Maseru

Durban

SOUTH AFRICA

Table Mountain

Great Karroo

Sheep

Cape Town

Zulu people

Car ship

Cape of Good Hope

Lobster

Kenyan children help to sort the coffee beans.

Bright beads

This Masai girl's headdress, earrings and collar are made from tiny beads. The children hold sticks for herding the family's cattle.

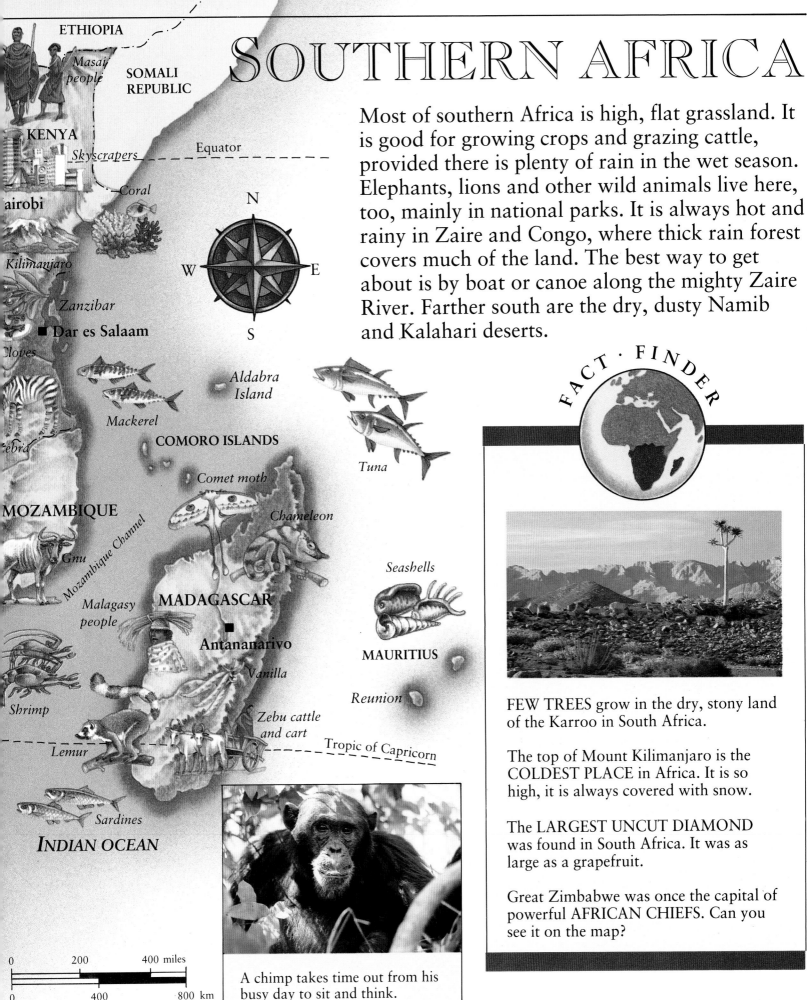

SOUTHERN AFRICA

Most of southern Africa is high, flat grassland. It is good for growing crops and grazing cattle, provided there is plenty of rain in the wet season. Elephants, lions and other wild animals live here, too, mainly in national parks. It is always hot and rainy in Zaire and Congo, where thick rain forest covers much of the land. The best way to get about is by boat or canoe along the mighty Zaire River. Farther south are the dry, dusty Namib and Kalahari deserts.

ETHIOPIA

Masai people

SOMALI REPUBLIC

KENYA

Skyscrapers

Equator

airobi

Coral

N

W   E

S

Kilimanjaro

Zanzibar

■ Dar es Salaam

Cloves

Aldabra Island

Mackerel

COMORO ISLANDS

Tuna

ebra

Comet moth

MOZAMBIQUE

Chameleon

Gnu

Mozambique Channel

Seashells

Malagasy people

MADAGASCAR

Antananarivo

MAURITIUS

Vanilla

Shrimp

Reunion

Lemur

Zebu cattle and cart

Tropic of Capricorn

Sardines

INDIAN OCEAN

0   200   400 miles

0   400   800 km

A chimp takes time out from his busy day to sit and think.

FEW TREES grow in the dry, stony land of the Karroo in South Africa.

The top of Mount Kilimanjaro is the COLDEST PLACE in Africa. It is so high, it is always covered with snow.

The LARGEST UNCUT DIAMOND was found in South Africa. It was as large as a grapefruit.

Great Zimbabwe was once the capital of powerful AFRICAN CHIEFS. Can you see it on the map?

CANADA

Most of Canada is a vast wilderness of ice and snow, forests and lakes. Many wild animals live here and in the Rocky Mountains, but few people can survive. Farmers herd cattle and grow huge fields of wheat on the grassy prairies east of the Rockies, but most people live in the big cities near the United States border.

A brown bear snatches a fish with its huge front paw.

Night sky spectacle

If you are quite far north or south on the Earth, you can sometimes see strange, colored lights in the night sky. These are known as *Aurora borealis* in the north and *Aurora australis* in the south.

ARCTIC OCEAN

Migrating king eider ducks

Beaufort Sea

Queen Elizabeth Islands

Alaska (US)

Arctic Circle

Icebreaker

Banks Island

Snowy owl

Mount Logan

Mackenzie

Pink lousewort

Victoria Island

Great Bear Lake

Arctic hare

YUKON TERRITORY

Mining (zinc)

Motor tricycles

NORTHWEST

Glaciers

Inuit (Eskimo)

Ice safari

Forestry

Great Slave Lake

Polar bear

Indian ceremonial mask

Cargo barges

BRITISH COLUMBIA

Peace

Moose

Herring

Oil

Reindeer Lake

Fraser

ALBERTA

Wheat

Nelson

Grizzly bear

Edmonton

MANITOBA

Salmon

Cattle

The Royal Canadian Mounted Police

Lake Winnipeg

Vancouver

Calgary

Perch

SASKATCHEWAN

Winnipeg

Vancouver Harbor

Calgary Stampede

THE UNITED STATES

Ice hockey

0	100	200	300	400	500 miles

0	200	400	600	800	1000 km

Ellesmere Island

evon land

Greenland

ICELAND

Baffin Bay

Caribou

Baffin Island

Icebergs

Arctic Circle

Davis Strait

TERRITORIES

Bowhead whale

Arctic buttercup

ATLANTIC OCEAN

Hudson Strait

Kittiwake

Bearded seal

Cod

Hudson Bay

Mining (iron ore)

Caribou

NEWFOUND-LAND

FACT · FINDER

Lake Superior is the LARGEST FRESHWATER LAKE in the world. Ships sail up the St. Lawrence River to the Great Lakes. How many lakes would you cross to reach Lake Superior? (Answer: p48)

The Inuits (Eskimos) have TWENTY different words for snow.

The CN Tower in Toronto is the TALLEST FREE-STANDING BUILDING in the world.

There are almost NO ROADS in northern Canada, so people use AIR TAXIS instead - small planes which can take off and land on the lakes.

Spruce grouse

Hydroelectric power

QUEBEC

Forestry

Cargo ship

Cabot tower

Fishing

ONTARIO

Forestry

Château Frontenac

Beaver

St. Lawrence

Ringed seal

Newfoundland

PRINCE EDWARD ISLAND

Lake Superior

Cargo ship

Lake Huron

Skiing

Quebec

NEW BRUNSWICK

Bald eagle

NOVA SCOTIA

Montreal

CN Tower

Ottawa

THE UNITED STATES

Scallops

ATLANTIC OCEAN

Beluga

Maple trees

Toronto

Lake Ontario

Lake Erie

Playing ice hockey is a good way to stay warm in the cold.

THE UNITED STATES

The United States of America is the fourth largest country in the world. It has thousands of miles of farmland, very hot deserts, and huge, snow-topped mountains. It also has some enormous cities. The giant of them all is New York City, home to over 7.3 million people.

FACT · FINDER

Huge SKYSCRAPERS tower above Manhattan in New York City. But the world's tallest skyscraper is found in a city on the edge of Lake Michigan. Can you see which one? (Answer: page 48)

About 250 MILLION PEOPLE live in the United States.

There are 50 STATES altogether. There is also a special piece of land, the District of Columbia. This is where the capital city, Washington, D.C., is found.

CANADA

Salmon
Boeing aircraft
Totem pole
Christmas trees
Greyhound bus
Olympia
WASHINGTON
Columbia
Salem
OREGON
Helena
MONTANA
Skiing
Forest products
Crater Lake
Boise
Yellowstone National Park
IDAHO
WYOMING
Mount Rushmo National Memc
Potatoes
Mining (gold)
Great Salt Lake
Mormon Temple
Coy
California redwood
Wine
NEVADA
Salt Lake City
Cheyenne
Sacramento
Carson City
Sagebrush
UTAH
Skiing
COLORADO
Denver
San Francisco
Gambling
Monument Valley
Rocky Mountains
Golden Gate Bridge
Fruit
Mesa Verde cliff dwellings
HOLLYWOOD
NEW MEXICO
Giant saguaro cactus
Santa Fe
Los Angeles
Colorado
Grand Canyon
PACIFIC OCEAN
Phoenix
ARIZONA
Cattle and sheep ranches
Oil and natural gas
Coral snake
MEXICO
Cattle and sheep ranches

THE RUSSIAN FEDERATION
ALASKA
Oil
Bering Strait
Motorized bobsleds
Arctic Circle
Yukon
CANADA
Mount McKinley
Forest products
Anchorage
0 100 200 300 miles
0 250 500 km
Kodiak bear

Alaska is much farther north than any of the other American states. It is a land of thick forests and high mountains. The winters are long and ice-cold, with snow covering much of the ground. The people often travel around in sleds or bobsleds.

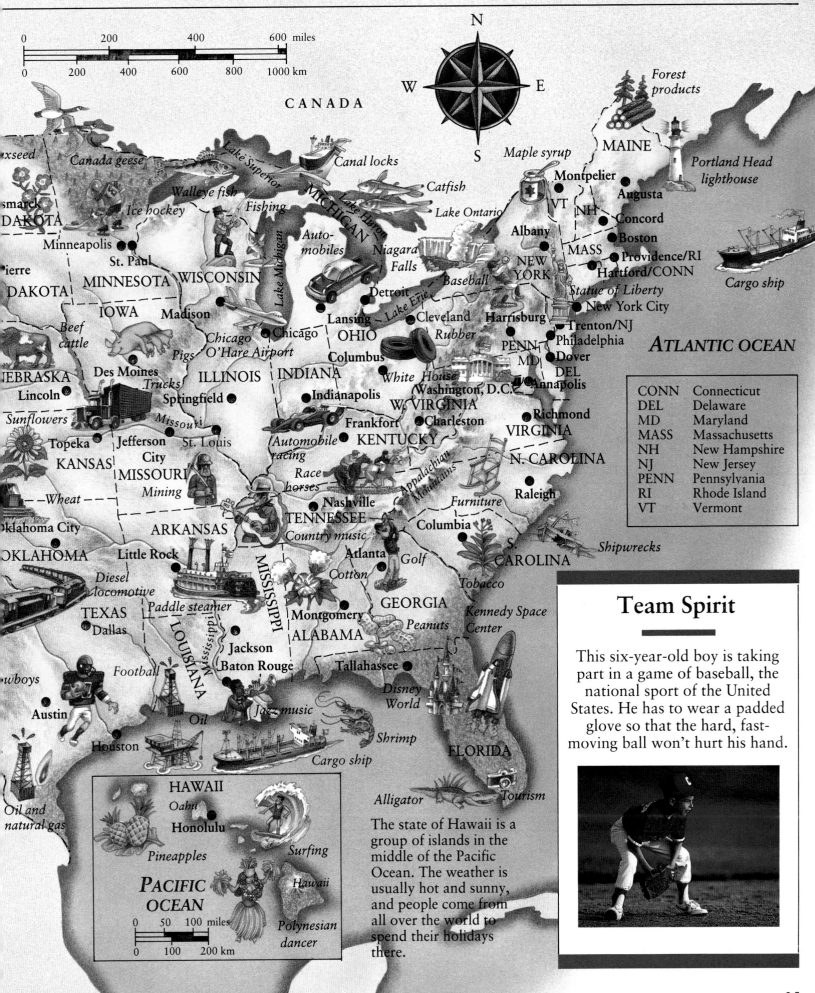

0   200   400   600 miles
0   200   400   600   800   1000 km

N
W E
S

CANADA

Forest products

Canada geese

Lake Superior   Canal locks

Maple syrup   MAINE

Catfish   Montpelier   Augusta   Portland Head lighthouse

Walleye fish   Lake Huron   Lake Ontario   VT   NH   Concord

Ice hockey   Fishing   MICHIGAN   Albany   Boston

xseed

smarck   DAKOTA

Minneapolis   St. Paul   Auto-mobiles   Niagara Falls   Baseball   NEW YORK   MASS   Providence/RI   Hartford/CONN

Pierre   DAKOTA   MINNESOTA   WISCONSIN   Lake Michigan   Detroit   Lake Erie   Statue of Liberty   New York City   Cargo ship

IOWA   Madison   Chicago   Cleveland   Harrisburg   Trenton/NJ

Beef cattle   Chicago   O'Hare Airport   Lansing   OHIO   Rubber   PENN   Philadelphia   ATLANTIC OCEAN

Pigs   Columbus   White House   MD   Dover

NEBRASKA   Des Moines   Trucks   ILLINOIS   INDIANA   Washington, D.C.   Annapolis   DEL

Lincoln   Springfield   Indianapolis   W. VIRGINIA

Sunflowers   Missouri   Frankfort   Charleston   Richmond

Topeka   Jefferson City   St. Louis   Automobile racing   KENTUCKY   VIRGINIA   N. CAROLINA

KANSAS   MISSOURI   Race horses   Appalachian Mountains   Raleigh

Wheat   Mining   Furniture

Oklahoma City   ARKANSAS   Nashville   TENNESSEE   Columbia   S. CAROLINA

OKLAHOMA   Little Rock   Country music   Atlanta   Golf   Shipwrecks

Diesel locomotive   MISSISSIPPI   Cotton   Tobacco

Paddle steamer   GEORGIA   Kennedy Space Center

TEXAS   Montgomery   Peanuts

Dallas   LOUISIANA   Jackson   ALABAMA   Tallahassee

Football   Baton Rouge   Disney World

cowboys   Oil   Jazz music   Shrimp

Austin   FLORIDA

Houston   Cargo ship

Oil and natural gas   Alligator   Tourism

CONN	Connecticut
DEL	Delaware
MD	Maryland
MASS	Massachusetts
NH	New Hampshire
NJ	New Jersey
PENN	Pennsylvania
RI	Rhode Island
VT	Vermont

Team Spirit

This six-year-old boy is taking part in a game of baseball, the national sport of the United States. He has to wear a padded glove so that the hard, fast-moving ball won't hurt his hand.

HAWAII
Oahu
Honolulu
Pineapples
PACIFIC OCEAN
Surfing
Hawaii
Polynesian dancer

0   50   100 miles
0   100   200 km

The state of Hawaii is a group of islands in the middle of the Pacific Ocean. The weather is usually hot and sunny, and people come from all over the world to spend their holidays there.

35

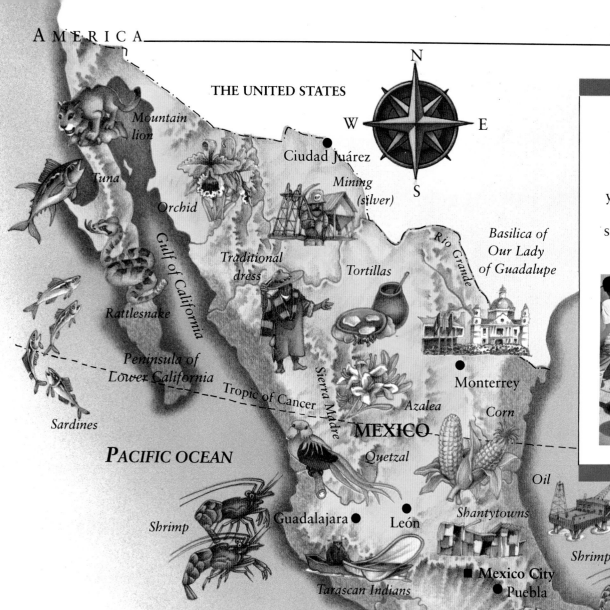

THE UNITED STATES

N
W E
S

Mountain lion

Tuna

Orchid

Gulf of California

Rattlesnake

Sardines

Peninsula of Lower California

Tropic of Cancer

PACIFIC OCEAN

Shrimp

Ciudad Juárez

Mining (silver)

Traditional dress

Tortillas

Sierra Madre

Quetzal

Rio Grande

Basilica of Our Lady of Guadalupe

Monterrey

Azalea

Corn

MEXICO

Shantytowns

Guadalajara

León

Tarascan Indians

Oil

Lobster

Shrimp

Mexico City

Puebla

Rain forest

Aztec ruins

Maya ruins

Traditional dress

BELIZE

Chur the V of Sorr

Belmopan

Rain forest

GUATEMALA

Guatemala

Tegucigalpa

EL SALVADOR

San Salvador

Mana

Coffee

On the beat

Steel drums are made from 55-gallon oil drums. This young musician has to know exactly where to hit the surface to get the right notes.

CENTRAL AMERICA AND THE WEST INDIES

Central America is a narrow strip of land connecting North and South America. It is an area that includes lush jungles as well as high mountains and hot deserts. Mexico is the largest country there. The West Indies are a group of islands that form a long curve in the sunny Caribbean Sea.

A jaguar sharpens its needle-like claws ready for the next hunt.

THE UNITED
STATES

Helping in a busy market
store is appetizing work.

The PANAMA CANAL is an
important shortcut for ships between
the Atlantic and Pacific oceans. Ships
that want to get from one ocean to
another can take this route instead of
having to sail right around the
bottom of South America. Up to
15,000 ships use the canal each year.
Can you see it on the map?

Mexico City is the LARGEST CITY
in the world, with over 19,000,000
people. This single city has a larger
population than any of the other
countries shown here.

BAHAMAS

Cigars

Coral
reef

Tourism

Tropic of Cancer

ATLANTIC
OCEAN

Havana

CUBA

Fishing

Fishing

Windsurfing

Sugar
cane

DOMINICAN
REPUBLIC

Puerto
Rico (US)

ANTIGUA &
BARBUDA

Lemons

HAITI

Cayman
Islands (UK)

Port-au-Prince

Santo Domingo

ST. KITTS-
NEVIS

St. John's

Sailing

JAMAICA

Kingston

Guadeloupe (France)

Waterskiing

Roseau

Sword
fish

DOMINICA

Crab

Martinique (France)

Lobster

ST. LUCIA

Castries

BARBADOS

Steel
band

Kingstown

HONDURAS

Caribbean Sea

ST. VINCENT &
THE GRENADINES

Bridgetown

Bananas

Containership

GRENADA

Netherlands
Antilles

St. George's

NICARAGUA

Cotton

Port-of-Spain

TRINIDAD
& TOBAGO

Lake
Nicaragua

Panama Canal

Traditional
dress

Golden
beaches

COSTA RICA

VENEZUELA

San José

PANAMA

Panama
City

COLOMBIA

Fishing

Monkey

0   200   400 miles

0   200   400   600 km

Parrot

37

SOUTH AMERICA

The continent of South America is over 7,500 km long. It stretches from the hot Equator to the icy seas that surround Antarctica. A huge tropical rain forest grows along and around the mighty Amazon River in the north. It is the largest rain forest in the world, covering about two-fifths of the continent.

Hanging Around

Two-toed sloths live in the Amazonian rain forest. They spend most of their time hanging upside down from the branches of trees. They can even sleep in this position.

N
E
S
W

Equator

Salvador
Maned wolf

Sugarcane
Boa constrictor

Giant toad

Portulaca flower

Rain forest clearing

Government buildings

Shrimp

Amazon

Piranha

Spider monkey

Brazil nuts

Armadillo

BRAZIL

Jaguar

FRENCH GUIANA
Cayenne
Paramaribo
SURINAM
Georgetown
GUYANA

Rice

Angel Falls

Amazon

Amazon

Blue and yellow macau

Bolivian

Oil

VENEZUELA
Caracas
Oil

Orinoco

Llanos

Lake Maracaibo

Bogotá
COLOMBIA

Mining (emeralds)
Coffee

Vampire bat

Amazon rain forest

Manatee

Selvas

Rubber

Amazonian

Reed boats

Andean condor

Inca ruins at Machu Picchu

Lake

Panpipes

PANAMA

Balsa tree

Equator

Quito
ECUADOR

Llama

Highest railway

ANDES

PERU
Lima

Anchovettas

38

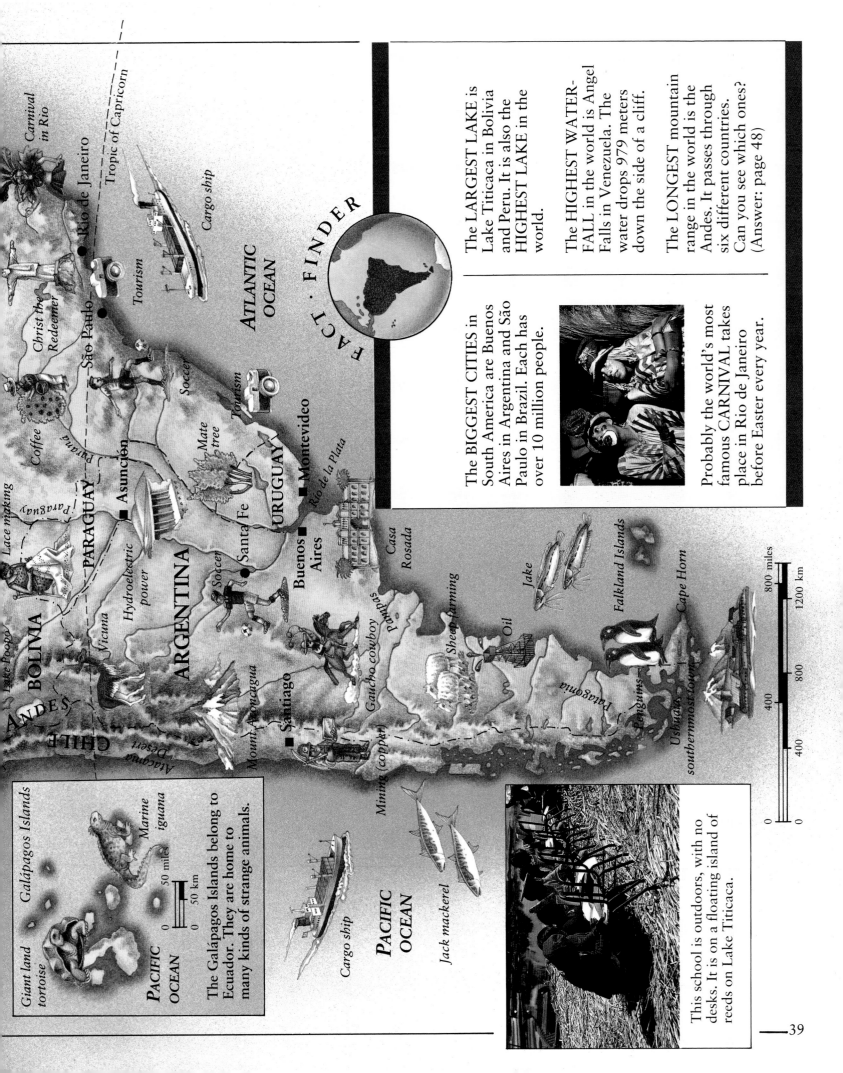

Carnival in Rio

Rio de Janeiro

Tropic of Capricorn

Cargo ship

Tourism

Christ the Redeemer

São Paulo

ATLANTIC OCEAN

Coffee

Lace making

Paraná

Paraguay

PARAGUAY

Asunción

Soccer

Mate tree

Tourism

Santa Fe

URUGUAY

Montevideo

Río de la Plata

Hydroelectric power

ARGENTINA

Soccer

Buenos Aires

Casa Rosada

Vicuña

Lake Poopó

BOLIVIA

ANDES

CHILE

Atacama Desert

Mount Aconcagua

Santiago

Gaucho cowboy

Pampas

Sheep farming

Oil

Lake

Falkland Islands

Patagonia

Penguins

Ushuaia southernmost town

Cape Horn

Mining (copper)

Cargo ship

PACIFIC OCEAN

Jack mackerel

0   400   800 miles
0   400   800   1200 km

FACT·FINDER

The LARGEST LAKE is Lake Titicaca in Bolivia and Peru. It is also the HIGHEST LAKE in the world.

The HIGHEST WATER-FALL in the world is Angel Falls in Venezuela. The water drops 979 meters down the side of a cliff.

The LONGEST mountain range in the world is the Andes. It passes through six different countries. Can you see which ones? (Answer: page 48)

The BIGGEST CITIES in South America are Buenos Aires in Argentina and São Paulo in Brazil. Each has over 10 million people.

Probably the world's most famous CARNIVAL takes place in Rio de Janeiro before Easter every year.

Galápagos Islands

Marine iguana

Giant land tortoise

0   50 miles
0   50 km

PACIFIC OCEAN

The Galápagos Islands belong to Ecuador. They are home to many kinds of strange animals.

This school is outdoors, with no desks. It is on a floating island of reeds on Lake Titicaca.

AUSTRALIA

The weather in Australia is often hot and dry. The center of the country is mainly desert, so most people live in towns and cities on the coast. Until about 200 years ago, only Aborigines lived there, but since then, people have come to settle from all over the world.

Aborigine children enjoying the rain after weeks of dry weather.

FACT · FINDER

Australia is both the SMALLEST continent and the LARGEST island in the world.

There are TEN TIMES more sheep than there are people in Australia. Some of the cattle herds are so enormous that the farmers use helicopters to help round them up.

The Aborigines call Ayers Rock *Uluru*. To them, it is a very SACRED PLACE. Many paintings and carvings, some of which are very old indeed, cover the walls of the caves inside it. Can you spot it on the map?

INDONESIA

N
W   E
S

Timor Sea

Shrimp

Kimberley

Baobab tree

Fitzroy

INDIAN OCEAN

Mining (bauxite)

Aborigine

Great Sandy Desert

Grass tree

Crocodile

Emu

Tropic of Capricorn

Desert death adder

Dingo

Spider orchid

WESTERN AUSTRALIA

Thorny devil

Schooling by radio

Sheep

Budgerig

Perth

Mining (gold)

Echidna

Lobster

Wandering albatrosses

SOUTHERN OCE

0   200   400 miles
0   200   400   600   800 km

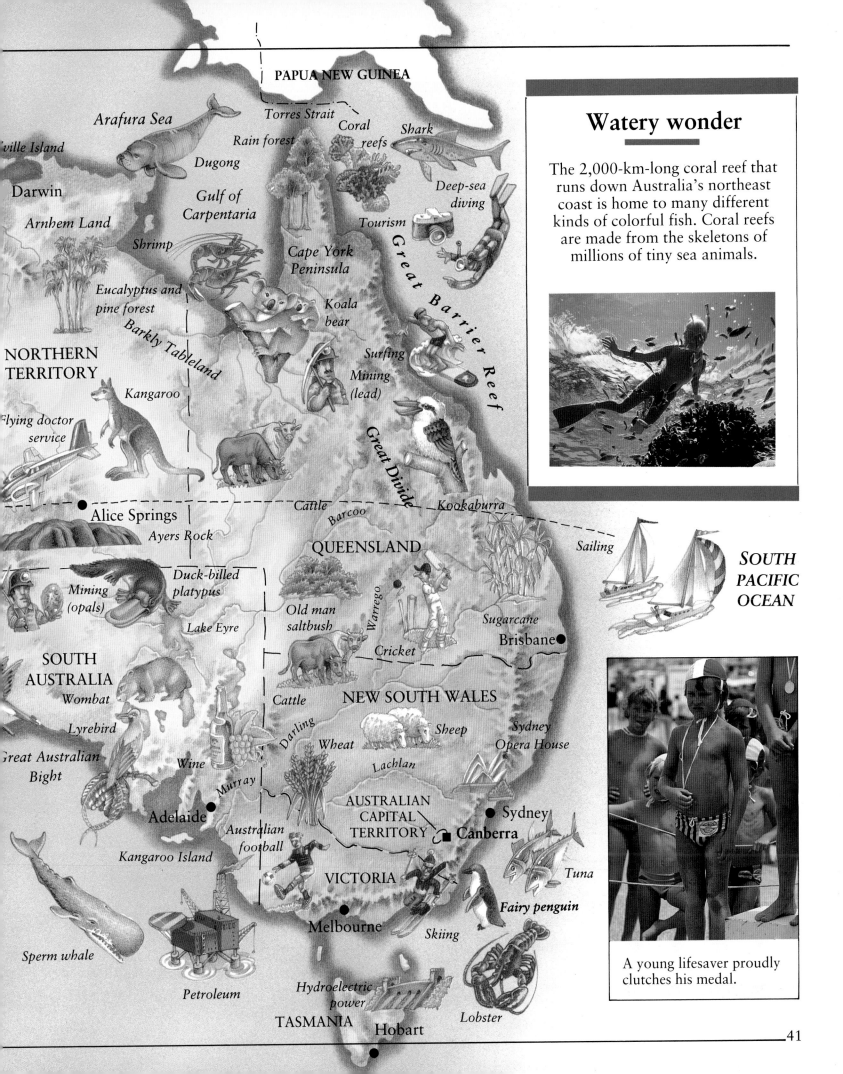

PAPUA NEW GUINEA

Arafura Sea

Torres Strait

Coral reefs

Shark

Rain forest

Dugong

...ville Island

Darwin

Gulf of Carpentaria

Deep-sea diving

Arnhem Land

Tourism

Shrimp

Cape York Peninsula

Eucalyptus and pine forest

Koala bear

NORTHERN TERRITORY

Barkly Tableland

Great Barrier Reef

Surfing

Mining (lead)

Kangaroo

Flying doctor service

Great Divide

Cattle

Barcoo

Kookaburra

Alice Springs

Sailing

Ayers Rock

QUEENSLAND

Mining (opals)

Duck-billed platypus

Old man saltbush

Sugarcane

SOUTH PACIFIC OCEAN

Lake Eyre

Warrego

Brisbane

SOUTH AUSTRALIA

Cricket

Wombat

Cattle

NEW SOUTH WALES

Lyrebird

Darling

Wheat

Sheep

Sydney Opera House

Great Australian Bight

Wine

Lachlan

Murray

Adelaide

AUSTRALIAN CAPITAL TERRITORY

Sydney

Australian football

Canberra

Tuna

Kangaroo Island

VICTORIA

Fairy penguin

Sperm whale

Melbourne

Skiing

Petroleum

Hydroelectric power

Lobster

TASMANIA

Hobart

Watery wonder

The 2,000-km-long coral reef that runs down Australia's northeast coast is home to many different kinds of colorful fish. Coral reefs are made from the skeletons of millions of tiny sea animals.

A young lifesaver proudly clutches his medal.

NEW ZEALAND AND THE PACIFIC

The Pacific Ocean covers nearly half of the world's surface. There are many thousands of islands dotted across its surface. The largest are New Guinea and the two islands of New Zealand. The rest are divided into groups that make up the different countries.

ASIA

N
W E
S

JAPAN

The Marianas Trench

Golden long-nosed butterfly fish

Midway I. (US)

Luxury liner

Coral atolls

Gold
b

Aircraft carrier

Northern Mariana Islands (US)
Coral

MARSHALL ISLANDS

Fishing with spears

Guam (US)

FEDERATED STATES OF MICRONESIA

Micronesian islander

Coconuts

THE PHILIPPINES

Koror
Palau (US)

Palikir

Dalap-Uliga-Darrit

Bananas

Princess Stephanie bird

Airplane routes

Equator

INDONESIA

Tuna

Houses on stilts

Bairiki

NAURU

Phosphate

Lobster

Lychees

PAPUA NEW GUINEA

Tourism

PO₄

TUVALU

SOLOMON ISLANDS
Honiara

Fongafale

Tokel. Is. N

Port Moresby

Pineapple

Wallis and Futuna (Fr)

WESTER SAMO

Forestry

VANUATU
Port-Vila

FIJI

Apia

TONG

Volcano

Suva

Nuku'al

New Caledonia (Fr)

Nouméa

Polynesian islander

AUSTRALIA

Tuna

Coral

Sheep

Kiwi

Auckland

Kiwi fruit

Wellington
NEW ZEALAND

Christchurch

Hooker sea lion

Maori

Garf

Anyone for cricket?

Cricket is a favorite sport in New Zealand. It was introduced by people from Britain who first settled there 200 years ago.

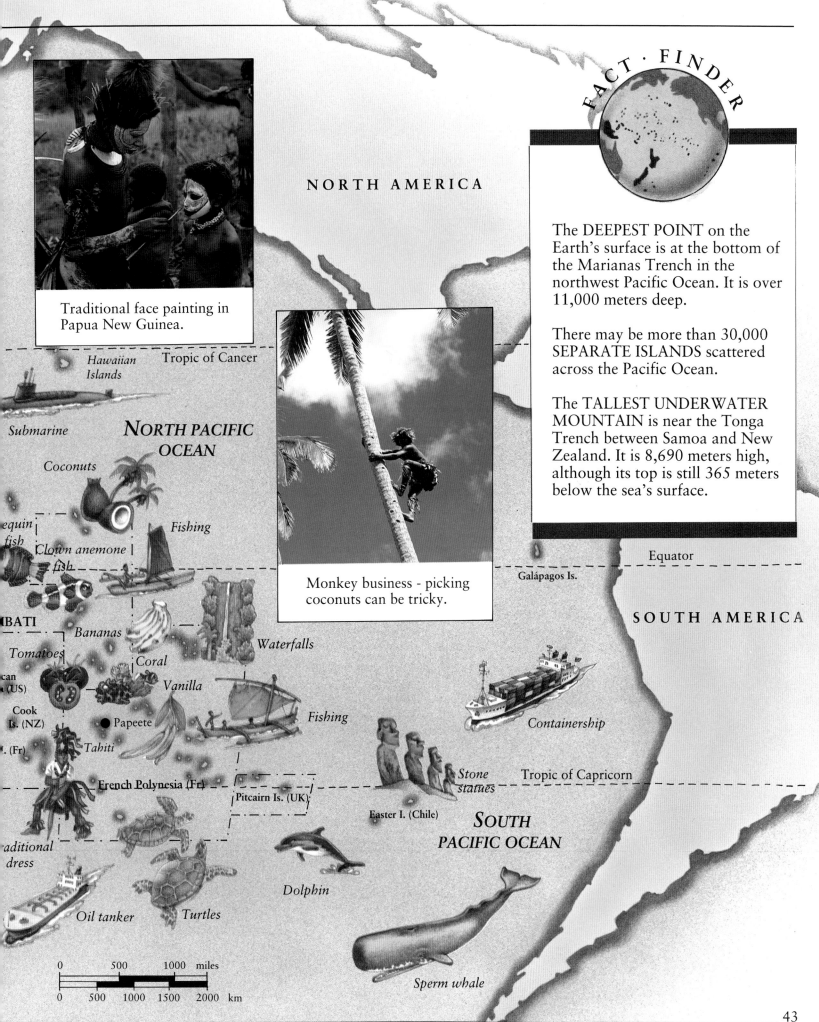

NORTH AMERICA

The DEEPEST POINT on the Earth's surface is at the bottom of the Marianas Trench in the northwest Pacific Ocean. It is over 11,000 meters deep.

There may be more than 30,000 SEPARATE ISLANDS scattered across the Pacific Ocean.

The TALLEST UNDERWATER MOUNTAIN is near the Tonga Trench between Samoa and New Zealand. It is 8,690 meters high, although its top is still 365 meters below the sea's surface.

Traditional face painting in Papua New Guinea.

Hawaiian Islands   Tropic of Cancer

Submarine

NORTH PACIFIC OCEAN

Coconuts

Fishing

equin fish

Clown anemone fish

Monkey business - picking coconuts can be tricky.

Equator

Galápagos Is.

SOUTH AMERICA

IBATI

Bananas

Tomatoes

Coral

Waterfalls

can (US)

Vanilla

Cook Is. (NZ)

● Papeete

Fishing

Containership

. (Fr)

Tahiti

Stone statues

Tropic of Capricorn

French Polynesia (Fr)

Pitcairn Is. (UK)

Easter I. (Chile)

SOUTH PACIFIC OCEAN

aditional dress

Dolphin

Oil tanker   Turtles

Sperm whale

0	500	1000	miles
0	500	1000	1500	2000	km

ANTARCTIC

Antarctica lies at the South Pole, the most southern point on Earth. It is always cold there, and a thick layer of ice covers the land. Few animals and plants can live on Antarctica itself, but the surrounding seas are full of life.

A research ship moves slowly through icy seas.

Blue whale

Elephant seal

Emperor penguin

Supply aircraft

ATLANTIC OCEAN

South Sandwich Is.

Sheathbill

Queen Maud Land

Flowering plant (Lyallia kerguelensis)

Icebergs

Southern lights (Aurora australis)

Albatross

Crabeater seal

South Orkney Is.

Antarctic Peninsula

Glacier

Antarctic Circle

Skua

Flowering plant (Oxalis enneaphylla)

Amundsen-Scott Research Station

Falkland Is.

South Pole

Mount Markham

South Magnetic Pole

Krill (shrimp)

INDIAN OCEAN

SOUTH AMERICA

Adélie penguins

Icebreaker

Gentoo penguin

Shipwreck

Polar explorer

Mount Erebus

Weddell seal

Giant petrel

McMurdo Station

Squid

Tasmania

FACT · FINDER

SOUTHERN OCEAN

AUSTRAL

Sit on Dad's feet - that's a really good way to keep warm.

Antarctica is the COLDEST PLACE on Earth. In 1983, a record low temperature of -128.6°F was recorded by Russian scientists.

The BIGGEST ICEBERG on record, sighted in the South Pacific Ocean, was 335 km long and 97 km wide. This is larger than the country of Belgium.

0	500	1000 miles

0	500	1000	1500	2000 km

ARCTIC

The Arctic is the area around the North Pole, the most northern point on Earth. There is no land there, only a floating island of ice. Like the Antarctic, the Arctic is very cold all year round.

These polar bear cubs have grown almost as big as their mother.

FACT · FINDER

The island of Greenland has the FASTEST-MOVING major glacier (river of ice) in the world. It flows about 24 meters each day.

The world's BEST FISHING GROUNDS lie around the Arctic area. The type of fish caught most often is shown on the map. Can you guess which one? (Answer: p.48)

PACIFIC OCEAN

Arctic Circle

Walrus

Arctic fox

Siberia

Containership

ASIA

Lemmings

Evergreen forests

Aircraft routes

Icebergs

ARCTIC OCEAN

Northern lights (Aurora borealis)

Ermine

Submarine

Krill (shrimp)

Arctic research station

Arctic Circle

Victoria I.

North Magnetic Pole

North Pole

Ellesmere I.

Polar bear

Svalbard

NORTH AMERICA

Thule

Inuit (Eskimo)

Cod

Saxifrage

Narwhal

Hudson Bay

Ptarmigan

GREENLAND

Evergreen forests

Baffin I.

Mining (cryolite)

Fishing

EUROPE

Godthaab

ICELAND

Caribou

Arctic char

Bearded seal

ATLANTIC OCEAN

Right whale

Walrus whiskers

The thick, bristly hairs on this walrus's upper lip are very sensitive to touch. They probably help it to search out the clams that it loves to eat.

Snowmobiles, not dogs, pull today's Eskimo sleds.

INDEX

A

Abidjan, 28
Abu Dhabi, 21
Abuja, 28
Accra, 28
Adana, 20
Addis Ababa, 29
Adelaide, 41
Aden, 21
Afghanistan, 11, 22
Africa, 5
    northern, 28-29
    southern, 30-31
Ahmadabad, 23
Alabama, 35
Alaska, 10, 34, 35
Albania, 10, 15
Albany, 35
Aleppo, 20
Alexandria, 29
Algeria, 11, 28-29
Algiers, 28
Alice Springs, 41
Alma-Ata, 18
America, 5, 32, 34, 36, 38
American Samoa, 43
Amman, 20
Amsterdam, 12
Anchorage, 34
Andaman Islands, 26
Andes Mountains, 38-39
Andorra, 10, 13
Angola, 11, 30
Ankara, 20
Annapolis, 35
Antananarivo, 31
Antarctica, 5, 7, 10, 44
Antigua & Barbuda,
    10, 37
Apia, 42
Appalachian Mountains,
    35
Arctic, 5, 7, 45
Argentina, 10, 39
Århus, 17
Arizona, 34
Arkansas, 35
Armenia, 11, 18
Ashkhabad, 18
Asia, 5, 22, 24, 26
Asmera, 29
Asunción, 39
Athens, 15
Atlanta, 35
Auckland, 42
Augusta, 35
Austin, 35
Australia, 5, 11, 40
Austria, 10, 13

Azerbaijan, 11, 18

B

Baghdad, 21
Bahamas, 10, 37
Bahrain, 11, 21
Bairiki, 42
Baku, 18
Balearic Islands, 13
Bali, 27
Baltic Sea, 17
Bamako, 28
Bandar Seri Begawan, 26
Bandung, 26
Bangalore, 23
Bangkok, 26
Bangladesh, 11, 23
Bangui, 29
Banjul, 28
Barbados, 10, 37
Barcelona, 13
Barnaul, 19
Baton Rouge, 35
Beirut, 20
Belarus, 11, 18
Belfast, 12
Belgium, 10, 12
Belgrade, 15
Belize, 10, 36
Belmopan, 36
Benin, 11, 28
Bergen, 17
Berlin, 12
Bern, 13
Bhutan, 11, 23
Bioko, 29
Bishkek, 18
Bismarck, 35
Bissau, 28
Bogotá, 38
Boise, 34
Bolivia, 38-39
Bombay, 23
Bonn, 12
Borneo, 27
Bornholm, 17
Bosnia-Herzegovina,
    10, 15
Bosporus, 15
Boston, 35
Botswana, 11, 30
Brasília, 38
Bratislava, 14
Brazil, 10, 38-39
Brazzaville, 30
Bridgetown, 37
Brisbane, 41
Brunei, 26

Brussels, 12
Bucharest, 15
Budapest, 14
Buenos Aires, 39
Bujumbura, 30
Bulgaria, 11, 14
Burkina Faso, 11, 28
Burundi, 11, 30

C

Cairo, 29
Calcutta, 23
Calgary, 32
California, 34
Cambodia (Kampuchea),
    11, 26
Cameroon, 11, 29
Canada, 10, 32-33
Canary Islands, 29
Canberra, 41
Cape Horn, 39
Cape of Good Hope, 30
Cape Town, 30
Cape Verde, 10
Caracas, 38
Caribbean Sea, 36, 37
Carson City, 35
Casablanca, 28
Castries, 37
Cayenne, 38
Cayman Islands, 37
Central African Republic,
    11, 29
Chad, 11, 29
Changchun, 25
Charleston, 35
Chelyabinsk, 18
Chengdu, 24
Cheyenne, 34
Chicago, 35
Chile, 10, 39
China, 8, 11, 24-25
Chios, 15
Chittagong, 23
Chongqing, 25
Christchurch, 42
Ciudad Juárez, 36
Cleveland, 35
Colombia, 10, 38
Colombo, 23
Colorado, 34
Columbia, 35
Columbus, 35
Comoro Islands, 31
Conakry, 28
Concord, 35
Congo, 11, 30
Connecticut, 35
Cook Islands, 43
Copenhagen, 17
Corfu, 15
Corsica, 13
Costa Rica, 10, 37
Crete, 15
Croatia, 10, 14

Cuba, 10, 37
Cyprus, 11, 21
Czech Republic, 10, 14

D

Dacca, 23
Dakar, 28
Dalap-Uliga-Darrit, 42
Dallas, 35
Damascus, 20
Dar es Salaam, 31
Dardanelles, 15
Darwin, 41
Delaware, 35
Denmark, 10, 17
Denver, 34
Des Moines, 35
desert, 6, 20
    Atacama, 39
    Gobi, 24
    Kalahari, 30
    Namib, 30
    Sahara, 28-29
    Taklimakan, 24
Detroit, 35
District of Columbia, 34
Djibouti, 11, 29
Doha, 21
Dominica, 10, 37
Dominican Republic,
    10, 37
Dover, 35
Dublin, 12
Dubrovnik, 15
Durban, 30
Dushanbe, 18
Dvina, 18

E

Easter I., 43
Ecuador, 10, 38
Edinburgh, 12
Edmonton, 32
Egypt, 11, 29
El Aaiún, 28
El Salvador, 10, 36
Ellesmere Island, 33
Equatorial Guinea, 11, 29
Eritrea, 11, 29
Estonia, 11, 18
Ethiopia, 11, 29
Europe, 5, 12, 14, 16

F

Fairbanks, 35
Falkland Islands, 39, 44
Fez, 28
Fiji, 11, 42
Finland, 10, 16, 17
Florida, 35
Fongafale, 42
France, 10, 12, 13
Frankfort, 35
Freetown, 28
French Guiana, 38

French Polynesia, 43

G

Gabon, 11, 30
Gaborone, 30
Galapagos Islands,
    39, 43
Gambia, 10, 28
Gdansk, 14
Georgetown, 38
Georgia, 11, 18
Georgia (US state), 35
Germany, 10, 12
Ghana, 11, 28
Glasgow, 12
Godthaab, 45
Göteborg, 17
Gotland, 17
Greece, 10, 14
Greenland, 10, 45
Grenada, 10, 37
Guadalajara, 36
Guadeloupe, 37
Guam, 42
Guangzhou, 25
Guatemala, 10, 36
Guatemala (city), 36
Guinea, 10, 28
Guinea-Bissau, 10, 28
Guyana, 10, 38

H

Hainan Island, 25
Haiti, 10, 37
Hamburg, 12
Hanoi, 26
Harare, 30
Harbin, 25
Harrisburg, 35
Hartford, 35
Havana, 37
Hawaii, 35, 43
Helena, 34
Helsinki, 17
Himalayas, 22, 23, 24
Ho Chi Minh City, 26
Hobart, 41
Hokkaido, 25
Honduras, 10, 37
Hong Kong, 25
Honiara, 43
Honolulu, 35
Honshu, 25
Houston, 35
Hudson Bay, 33
Hungary, 10, 15
Hyderabad, 23

I

Ibiza, 13
Iceland, 10, 16
Idaho, 34
Illinois, 35
India, 11, 22-23
Indiana, 35

Indianapolis, 35
Indonesia, 11, 26-27
Iowa, 35
Iran, 11, 21
Iraq, 11, 21
Ireland, Republic of,
    10, 12
Irian Jaya, 27
Irkutsk, 19
Isfahan, 21
Islamabad, 22
Israel, 11, 20
Istanbul, 20
Italy, 10
Ivory Coast, 11, 28
Izmir, 20

J

Jackson, 35
Jakarta, 26, 27
Jamaica, 10, 37
Japan, 11, 25
Java, 27
Jefferson City, 35
Jerusalem, 20
Jidda, 20
Johannesburg, 30
Jordan, 11, 20

K

Kabul, 22
Kaliningrad, 18
Kampala, 30
Kansas, 35
Karachi, 23
Kashmir, 22
Kathmandu, 23
Kazakhstan, 11, 18
Kentucky, 35
Kenya, 11, 30
Khabarovsk, 19
Kharkov, 18
Khartoum, 29
Kiev, 18
Kigali, 30
Kingston, 37
Kingstown, 37
Kinshasa, 30
Kiribati, 11, 43
Kishinev, 18
Kobe, 25
Koror, 42
Kraków, 14
Krasnoyarsk, 19
Kuala Lumpur, 26
Kuril Islands, 19
Kuwait, 11, 21
Kyoto, 25
Krygystan, 11, 18
Kyushu, 25

L

La Paz, 38
Lagos, 28
Lahore, 22

Lake
    Baikal, 18
    Chad, 29
    Erie, 33, 35
    Huron, 33, 35
    Malawi, 30
    Michigan, 35
    Nasser, 28
    Ontario, 33, 35
    Superior, 33, 35
    Tanganyika, 30
    Titicaca, 38
    Victoria, 30
    Winnipeg, 32
Lansing, 35
Laos, 11, 26
Las Palmas, 28
Latvia, 11, 18
Lebanon, 11, 20
León, 36
Lesbos, 15
Lesotho, 11, 30
Liberia, 10, 28
Libreville, 30
Libya, 11, 29
Liechtenstein, 10, 13
Lille, 12
Lilongwe, 30
Lima, 38
Lincoln, 35
Lisbon, 13
Lithuania, 11, 18
Little Rock, 35
Ljubljana, 14
Lodz, 14
Lofoten Islands, 17
Lomé, 28
London, 12
Los Angeles, 34
Louisiana, 35
Luanda, 30
Lulea, 16
Lusaka, 30
Luxembourg, 10, 12
Lyons, 13

M

Macao, 25
Macedonia, 10
Madagascar, 11, 31
Madison, 35
Madras, 23
Madrid, 13
Maine, 35
Malabo, 29
Malawi, 11, 30
Malaysia, 11, 26
Male, 23
Mali, 11, 28
Malmö, 17
Malta, 10, 29
Managua, 36
Manama, 21
Manchuria, 25
Manila, 27

Maputo, 30
Marrakesh, 28
Marseille, 13
Marshall Islands, 42
Martinique, 37
Maryland, 35
Maseru, 30
Massachusetts, 35
Mauritania, 10, 28
Mauritius, 31
Mbabane, 30
Medan, 26
Melbourne, 41
Meshed, 21
Mexico, 10, 36
Mexico City, 36
Michigan, 35
Middle East, 20
Milan, 13
Minneapolis, 35
Minnesota, 35
Minsk, 18
Mississippi, 35
Missouri, 35
Mogadishu, 29
Moldova, 10, 18
Moluccas, 27
Monaco, 10, 13
Mongolia, 11, 24-25
Monrovia, 28
Montana, 34
Monterrey, 36
Montevideo, 39
Montgomery, 35
Montpelier, 35
Montreal, 33
Morocco, 11, 28
Moscow, 18
Mount Everest, 22
Mozambique, 11, 30-31
Munich, 12
Murmansk, 18
Muscat, 21
Myanmar (Burma), 11, 26

N

N'Djamena, 29
Nagoya, 25
Nairobi, 31
Namibia, 11, 30
Nanjing, 25
Naples, 13
Nashville, 35
Nauru, 11, 42
Nebraska, 35
Nepal, 11, 22, 23
Netherlands Antilles, 37
Netherlands, The, 10, 12
Nevada, 34
New Caledonia, 42
New Delhi, 23
New Hampshire, 35
New Jersey, 35
New Mexico, 34
New York (state), 35

New York City, 34, 35
New Zealand, 11, 42
Niamey, 28
Nicaragua, 10, 37
Niger, 11, 28-29
Nigeria, 11, 28-29
Nizhni Novgorod, 18
North Carolina, 35
North Dakota, 35
North Korea, 11, 25
North Pole, 5, 45
Northern Mariana Is., 42
Norway, 10, 16, 17
Nouakchott, 28
Nouméa, 42
Novaya Zemlya, 19
Novokuznetsk, 19
Nuku'alofa, 42

O

Ohio, 35
Oklahoma, 35
Oklahoma City, 35
Öland, 17
Olympia, 34
Oman, 11, 21
Omsk, 18
Oregon, 34
Osaka, 25
Oslo, 17
Ottawa, 33
Ouagadougou, 28

P

Pakistan, 11, 22, 23
Palau, 42
Palikir, 42
Panama, 10, 37
Panama City, 37
Papeete, 43
Papua New Guinea,
    11, 42
Paraguay, 10, 39
Paramaribo, 38
Paris, 12
Pennsylvania, 35
Perth, 40
Peru, 10, 38
Philadelphia, 35
Philippines, The, 11, 27
Phnom Penh, 26
Phoenix, 34
Pierre, 35
Pitcairn Is., 43
Poland, 10, 14
Port Moresby, 42
Port-au-Prince, 37
Port-of-Spain, 37
Port-Vila, 42
Porto, 13
Porto-Novo, 28
Portugal, 10, 13
Prague, 14
Pretoria, 30
Providence, 35

Puebla, 36
Puerto Rico, 37
Pyongyang, 25

Q

Qatar, 11, 21
Quebec, 33
Quezon City, 26
Quito, 38

R

Rabat, 28
Raleigh, 35
Rangoon, 26
Reunion, 31
Reykjavik, 16
Rhode Island, 35
Rhodes, 15
Richmond, 35
Riga, 18
Rio de Janeiro, 39
river
    Amazon, 38
    Colorado, 34
    Danube, 14
    Ganges, 23
    Limpopo, 30
    Mekong, 27
    Mississippi, 35
    Missouri, 35
    Nile, 28
    Rio Grande, 36
    St. Lawrence, 33
    Zaire, 30
    Zambezi, 30
Riyadh, 21
Rocky Mountains, 34
Romania, 10, 14
Rome, 13
Roseau, 37
Rostov, 18
Rotterdam, 12
Rub'al Khali, 21
Russian Federation, The
    11, 18, 19
Rwanda, 11, 30

S

Sacramento, 34
Salem, 34
Salt Lake City, 34
Salvador, 39
Samara, 18
Samos, 15
San Francisco, 34
San José, 37
San Marino, 10, 13
San Salvador, 36
San'a, 21
Santa Fe, 34, 39
Santiago, 39
Santo Domingo, 37
São Paulo, 39
São Tomé & Principe,
    11, 30

Sapporo, 25
Sarajevo, 15
Sardinia, 13
Saudi Arabia, 11, 20-21
Semarang, 26
Senegal, 10, 28
Seoul, 25
Shanghai, 9, 25
Shenyang, 25
Shikoku, 25
Shiraz, 21
Siberia, 18, 19
Sicily, 13
Sierra Leone, 10, 28
Singapore, 11, 26
Skopje, 15
Slovakia, 10, 14
Slovenia, 10, 14
Sofia, 15
Solomon Islands, 11, 42
Somali Republic, 11, 29
South Africa, 11, 30
South Carolina, 35
South Dakota, 35
South Korea, 11, 25
South Orkney Is., 44
South Pole, 5, 44
South Sandwich Is., 44
Spain, 10, 13
Springfield, 35
Sri Lanka, 11, 23
St. George's, 37
St. John's, 37

St. Kitts-Nevis, 10, 37
St. Louis, 35
St. Lucia, 10, 37
St. Paul, 35
St. Petersburg, 18
St. Vincent & The
   Grenadines, 10, 37
Stockholm, 17
Sudan, 11, 29
Sulawesi (Celebes), 27
Sumatra, 27
Surabaya, 26
Surinam, 10, 38
Suva, 42
Svalbard, 45
Swaziland, 11, 30
Sweden, 10, 16, 17
Switzerland, 10, 13
Sydney, 41
Syria, 11, 20

T
Tabriz, 21
Tadzhikistan, 11, 18
Tahiti, 43
Taipei, 25
Taiwan, 25
Taiyuan, 25
Tallahassee, 35
Tallinn, 18
Tampere, 17
Tanzania, 11, 30-31
Tashkent, 18

Tasmania, 41
Tbilisi, 18
Tegucigalpa, 36
Teheran, 21
Tennessee, 35
Texas, 35
Thailand, 11, 26
Thessaloníki, 15
Thimbu, 23
Thule, 45
Tianjin, 25
Tibet, 24
Timor, 27
Tiranë, 15
Togo, 11, 28
Tokelau Is., 42
Tokyo, 9, 25
Tonga, 11, 43
Topeka, 35
Toronto, 33
Trenton, 35
Trinidad & Tobago, 10, 37
Tripoli, 29
Tunis, 29
Tunisia, 11, 29
Turin, 13
Turkey, 11, 20, 21
Turkmenistan, 11, 18
Turku, 17
Tuvalu, 11, 42

U
Ufa, 18

Uganda, 11, 30
Ukraine, 11, 18
Ulan Bator, 25
Ulan-Ude, 19
Umeå, 17
United Arab Emirates,
   11, 21
United Kingdom, 10, 12
United States,
   10, 34-35
Uruguay, 10, 39
Utah, 34
Uzbekistan, 11, 18

V
Vancouver, 32
Vanuatu, 11, 42
Vatican City, 10, 13
Venezuela, 10, 38
Venice, 13
Vermont, 35
Vienna, 12
Vientiane, 26
Vietnam, 11, 26
Vilnius, 18
Virginia, 35
Vladivostok, 19
Volgograd, 18

W
Wallis & Futuna, 42
Warsaw, 14
Washington, D.C., 35

Washington (state), 34
Wellington, 42
Western Sahara, 10, 28
Western Samoa, 11, 42
West Indies, 36
West Virginia, 35
Windhoek, 30
Winnipeg, 32
Wisconsin, 35
Wuhan, 25
Wyoming, 34, 35

X
Xi'an, 25

Y
Yangtze, 25
Yaoundé, 29
Yekaterinburg, 18
Yemen, 11, 21
Yerevan, 18
Yokohama, 25
Yugoslavia, 10, 15

Z
Zagreb, 14
Zaire, 11, 30
Zambia, 11, 30
Zanzibar, 31
Zhengzhou, 25
Zibo, 25
Zimbabwe, 11, 30
Zurich, 13

QUIZ ANSWERS

p.20   The hottest capital city in the world is Riyadh, in Saudi Arabia.
p.22   The Ganges River ends on the coast of Bangladesh, and empties into the Bay of Bengal.
p.27   The island of Borneo has parts of Indonesia and Malaysia, as well as the whole of Brunei.
p.34   The world's tallest skyscraper is in the city of Chicago.
p.45   The fish caught most often in Arctic waters is the cod.

ACKNOWLEDGEMENTS

The Publisher would like to thank the following for their kind permission to reproduce the photographs in this book:
Bryan and Cherry Alexander Back jacket bottom right, 18, 32 center and bottom, 45 bottom right;
Ardea/Jean-Paul Ferrero 8 left; /**Francois Gohier** 45 top; /**Nick Gordon** 36 bottom; /**C Clem Haagner** 29 left; /**Edwin Mickleburgh** 44 bottom; /**Ron and Valerie Taylor** 41 top; /**Adrian Warren** 7 bottom right, 31 left;
Robert Harding Picture Library /**Advertasia** 26; /**Tom Ang** 20 bottom; /**David Beatty** 19; /**Bildagentur Schuster** 13 center, 16 top left, 44 top; /**Nigel Blythe** 24 right; /**N A Callow** 12; /**Fin Costello** 13 top; /**Rob Cousins** 31 right; /**William Cremin** 36 top; /**Robert Estall** 33; /**Explorer** 14; /**Explorer/J P Nacivet** 7 bottom left; **Explorer/Tetrel** 28; /**Robert Freck** 37; /**Paul Freestone** 6 bottom; /**Ken Gillham** 9 bottom left, 24 left; /**Robert Harding** 6 center, 21 top; /**Hart** 16 bottom right; /**G Hellier** 23 top; /**Carol Jopp** 41 bottom; /**R McLeod** 8 bottom right; /**Tim Megarry** 8 top right; /**Bill O'Connor** 1, 30 bottom; /**Photri** 30 center; /**David Poole** Back jacket top left, 20 center, 29 right; /**Walter Rawlings** 13 bottom; /**Geoff Renner** 7 top; /**Sybil Sassoon** 22 top and bottom, 43 top left; /**Adina Tovy** 9 bottom right, 34; /**Dr A C Waltham** 6 top; /**Lia White** 43 center; /**J H C Wilson** 23 bottom; /**Loraine Wilson** 15; /**Adam Woolfit** Back jacket bottom left, 21 bottom, 42;
The Hutchison Library /**M MacIntyre** 27 center;
Impact Photos 27 top;
Rex Features Back jacket top right, 40;
South America Pictures/Tony Morrison 38, 39 bottom;
Tony Stone Worldwide 4, 39 top; /**Don Spiro** 35

EQUATORIAL GUINEA	ERITREA	ETHIOPIA	GAMBIA	GHANA
GUINEA	GUINEA-BISSAU	IVORY COAST	LIBERIA	LIBYA
MALI	MAURITANIA	MOROCCO	NIGER	NIGERIA
SÃO TOMÉ & PRINCIPE	SENEGAL	SIERRA LEONE	SOMALI REPUBLIC	SUDAN
TOGO	TUNISIA	WESTERN SAHARA	ANGOLA	BOTSWANA
BURUNDI	COMORO ISLANDS	CONGO	GABON	KENYA
LESOTHO	MADAGASCAR	MALAWI	MAURITIUS	MOZAMBIQUE
NAMIBIA	RWANDA	SEYCHELLES	SOUTH AFRICA	SWAZILAND
TANZANIA	UGANDA	ZAIRE	ZAMBIA	ZIMBABWE
CANADA	UNITED STATES OF AMERICA	ANTIGUA & BARBUDA	BAHAMAS	BARBADOS